THE RED TAIL

The
RED TAIL

Sharing the Seasons
with a Hawk

DANIEL BUTLER

Jonathan Cape
London

First published 1994

1 3 5 7 9 10 8 6 4 2

© Daniel Butler 1994

Daniel Butler has asserted his right
under the Copyright, Designs and Patents Act, 1988
to be identified as the author of this work

Illustrations by Sally Ashburton

First published in the United Kingdom in 1994 by
Jonathan Cape
Random House, 20 Vauxhall Bridge Road, London SW1V 2SA

Random House Australia (Pty) Limited
20 Alfred Street, Milsons Point, Sydney,
New South Wales 2061, Australia

Random House New Zealand Limited
18 Poland Road, Glenfield,
Auckland 10, New Zealand

Random House South Africa (Pty) Limited
PO Box 337, Bergvlei, South Africa

Random House UK Limited Reg. No. 954009

A CIP catalogue record for this book
is available from the British Library

ISBN 0-224-03867-2

Printed in Great Britain by
Clays Ltd, St. Ives PLC

Contents

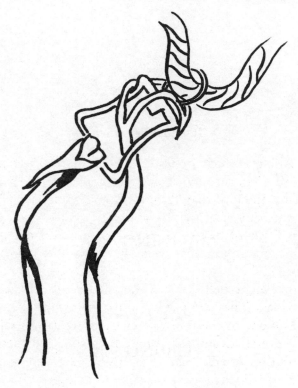

Jesses, swivel and leash

Glossary

Aylmeri   Anklets which are fastened with an eye-rivet around the bird's leg, through which a buttoned jess is threaded. Safer for the bird than traditional jesses, these are named after their inventor, Guy Aylmer.

Austringer   Flyer of hawks, as opposed to a falconer which, to the purist, means someone who flies longwings (falcons).

Bells   Lightweight bells that are attached to a hawk's legs and/or tail. They are used to trace the bird.

Cast   This is one of the most overworked words in falconry with several meanings, although fortunately these that the context usually clears confusion. To cast a bird is either to launch it into the air; or to immobilise it by holding its wings to its body so that routine chores, such as replacing aylmeri, can be performed. Alternatively, when the bird itself casts, it is disgorging a ball of undigested material from its crop. Similarly, 'casting' is food which will generate a pellet (also known as *a* casting). Finally, a cast can be a pair of birds flown together: traditionally peregrines at tough or difficult quarry such as rooks, geese or magpies; but nowadays most frequently a pair or more of the gregarious Harris hawks.

Creance A long, very light line, tied to the hawk's jesses during early training, before the falconer has the confidence to let the bird fly free.

Corvid Member of the crow family – rooks, jackdaws and magpies.

Entering Introducing the hawk to quarry – the final stage of training.

Eyass This has more than one meaning. It is a young hawk still in or around the nest sight, a bird taken for falconry from the nest (as opposed to trapped later) or, in today's falconry, a young captive-bred bird.

Falcon At its broadest it is any member of the genus *Falco* – raptors with long, pointed wings which usually prey on other birds. More specifically it is a female longwing and, at its most precise, it is a female peregrine.

Gyr Pronounced 'jer', this is the largest falcon in the world, its range extending around the Arctic circle. For centuries it has been regarded as the most impressive falconry bird, although until recently this seems to have been linked more to its size and beauty than performance in the field. Modern falconers, however – and particularly Americans – seem to have rediscovered its abilities.

Hack The process where an eyass is allowed to fly free and unsupervised to develop its muscles before being recaptured for training.

Haggard A hawk captured in adult plumage. Traditionally the most valued birds, the trapping of adults is now illegal in most countries.

Harris hawk Probably the most popular hunting bird in Britain today, these originate from central America and, although the sole members of a genus in their own right, they are closer to the buzzard than anything else.

Hawk Like falcon, this has more than one meaning. At its broadest it is any bird which kills for a living (from eagles to falcons) and at its narrowest it is just the shortwinged members of the genus *Accipiter* – such as goshawks and sparrowhawks. Matters are complicated by the early American settlers confusing terminologies and calling their buzzards 'hawks' and their vultures 'buzzards'. As a result the 'red tailed hawk' is really 'a red tailed buzzard'.

Hood Light leather blindfold used to calm the hawk and hide distressing or tempting sights from it. Vital in the training of falcons, it is of less use with hawks and rarely used with the very tranquil buzzards.

Jess(es) The leather straps that traditionally are tied around the bird's legs, but today tend to have a button at one end which is threaded through the eyelet of an Aylmeri anklet. The use of Aylmeri allows two types of jesses to be used – *mews jesses* which are slitted for use with a swivel and *field jesses* for use when the bird is flying free. These have no slit and therefore are unlikely to snag on obstructions, potentially to the danger of the hawk. Better still, if the bird does escape or is lost, it can pull out the buttoned strips, eliminating the risk of getting tangled up.

Leash The cord which slips through the swivel and is used to tie the hawk to its perch.

Manning The first stage of training a hawk, where it becomes used to human company.

Mews Indoor quarters for the hawk, used at night, for moulting and in bad weather.

Musket Male sparrowhawk.

Passager In theory a bird trapped on a migration route, but in practice often used to describe a bird caught but before it has moulted into adult plumage at the end of its first year.

Peregrine The largest British falcon and traditionally regarded as the pinnacle of European falconry.

Saker Large falcon from central Asia, particularly highly rated by Arab falconers. Some people believe it to be a subspecies of the Arctic gyr.

Swivel Made of two linked metal loops which can turn independently of each other and which are used to link the jesses to the leash. It ensures that the hawk does not get tangled up on its perch.

Spar Sparrowhawk

Stoop To plummet down from a height on prey. A hunting technique employed particularly by falcons and of which the peregrine is probably the supreme exponent.

Telemetry Radio tracking devices used to trace hawks, particularly the far-flying falcons or the more highly-strung species.

Tiercel A male peregrine, but also used as 'tiercel goshawk' to describe the male of that species. So named because the male peregrine is about a third smaller than the female (this divergence in size applies to most diurnal birds of prey).

Weathering The place where a hawk is tethered during daylight hours to get fresh air and to bathe.

Yarak In peak hunting condition, both physically and psychologically. Originally a Turkish word, it is most usually applied to goshawks.

Part One

MANNING

Friday 9 October

HE ARRIVED THIS morning, three hours earlier than expected. The small cardboard box was less glamorous and impressive than I had somehow imagined and when I took it gingerly from the delivery man, it was lighter too. My breath came out in puffs. Frost dusted the bushes and I was still half-asleep, exhausted after a short night. I had returned to Oxfordshire from London late last night, worn out from a day working in an ITN office. Knowing of his imminent arrival, but still not fully prepared, I stayed up late, fumbling with leather and astro-turf, books strewn across the kitchen table, desperately trying to make sure everything was ready.

And all the while I was worrying if there was any way in which I could fit a pair of bells without someone else to hold the unhappy arrival. Of course I couldn't. Hence my foggy welcome as the van's doors swung open and the box emerged.

'He' was a red-tailed buzzard, fresh from a Norfolk breeder, and he represented the culmination of twenty years of daydreams.

It had begun at the age of ten.

I was playing in the cottage garden with a friend when something made me suggest a walk. I don't know why, but

I decided we should venture into a field that we normally left well alone, one immediately behind the house of a particularly unfriendly local farmer. It was a fateful walk. We found a kestrel with a sprained wing. As she stood on the ground staring back at me intently, I realised something was wrong, a realisation that was only confirmed as I chased her around the nettle beds without forcing her to take wing. Eventually cornered, she rolled on to her back, kicking out with her feet, her tiny frame filled with enough hatred and pluck to dare me to take her on. But I was determined and, by throwing my jersey over the thrashing talons, I conquered her.

I carried her back to the cottage, heart pounding. In retrospect, just one look had done the damage. Instead of displaying my manhood by 'putting it out of its misery', as I would probably have dealt with a blackbird or pigeon, I had to keep this bird alive. I was hooked.

A visit to a local falconer produced some basic information. As my father and I stood blinking in his kitchen at midnight, he suggested gently that he should take the bird, but I was adamant, as defiant as the kestrel. Sighing softly, he examined the wing and diagnosed a bad sprain. He gave us the name of a vet who specialised in birds, fitted jesses – the slitted leather straps that wrap around the bird's legs – and lent me a swivel and perch. Before we left, he showed me his own birds – two peregrines and a breeding pair of red tails. I had no time for them. My interest was concentrated on the kestrel. Smiling, he wished us goodnight.

The injured bird stayed in the back garden for three weeks, tethered to a perch and fed on butcher's meat, until one dreadful day she picked her leash undone and flew off – almost certainly to die hanging upside down, tangled in the branches of a tree.

For weeks afterwards I scoured the skies for her silhouette: pointed wings, long thin tail and, to my shame, trailing behind the thread of the leash. Although I learned rapidly to distinguish the flight of a kestrel from a woodpigeon, a thrush from a sparrowhawk, I saw her only twice more – each time well out of reach of my despairing entreaties. Why, after all, should she come back to me from a tree when I had never persuaded her to hop from a post to my fist?

Yet, in spite of the blatant failure of my clumsy efforts to tame this diminutive mouse-killer, I had been bitten, inoculated with an obsession and the desperate desire to have another hawk of my own. Hobbies normally come and go: most of us can chart our teen years through the half-forgotten memories of each year's passion, but for the rest of my school days and throughout my twenties this dream stayed with me.

First I acquired ferrets. Then a dog. Airguns, cars, alcohol and the question of virginity all came and went. I left home, went to university and got a job, but still the thought of owning a hawk was there, lurking deep in my mind, to reappear sporadically, triggered by the sight of a motorway kestrel, a soaring buzzard or a hunting owl. Every six months or so, I'd pause at the bookshelf, see one of my falconry books and pull it down, blowing the dust off its cover. I had half a dozen, but the most battered was T. H. White's classic, *The Goshawk*. From the age of ten to twenty-eight, I read it every summer, following his struggles, tutting at his ignorance, wincing at his mistakes, but all the time envious. To own a goshawk! Dreams of the bird sent me to sleep throughout my school years, at university and even, I remember, the night before I moved into my first house. I'd drift into unconsciousness, my mind filled with the goshawk: of the rabbits and hares we'd catch and the impressive figure I'd cut striding across fields with the brooding bird on my outstretched left fist.

Sometimes, when no one was looking, I'd even stand in the kitchen, a gardening glove on my hand, balancing a bag of sugar or flour on the fist, imagining what it would feel like. How long could one keep one's arm at a right angle with a couple of pounds at the end? One particularly boring physics lesson I even calculated the forces involved – but of course the result, if not the motive, is long since lost.

I never got one. At university there was nowhere to keep it and when I began to work I imagined myself progressing too far and fast to make it practical. But then life changed again. I was made redundant and the trainee journalist on a business magazine became a freelance, answerable to no one but himself.

The first real steps towards possessing a hawk began, however, with the pregnancy of one of my dogs. As the other entered a second childhood and became increasingly incontinent, I mated the younger with a neighbouring collie. Two dogs are, in many ways, less trouble than one, and I wanted to keep a puppy to replace the ancient Sian who clearly hadn't long to go.

After a trouble-free nine weeks, seven mongrel puppies appeared under the stairs of my Islington flat. Friends might regard me as mildly eccentric, but plain unsanitary I am not. As the pups reached three weeks and began to spill out of their basket, the thought of spending a long hot summer cramped in a two-bedroom flat with nine dogs, eight of which lacked housetraining, was too much. I decamped to my parents' Oxfordshire cottage and the puppies were banished to an outhouse.

My stay was meant to be for a month or so, but as time went on I realised how much I liked being on my own in the countryside. Better still, with my parents away in America on sabbatical, it was clear that I could not only stay for a year if I wanted, but that I did indeed want to. It was at this point that I spotted *The Goshawk* again, as dusty as ever, the gold lettering on its battered red covers barely legible. Picking it up I began to read and once more the old dreams came back on their annual jaunt, but with a difference. For the first time in twenty years, I knew the answer was 'yes'.

For months I read and re-read the manuals. They were divided in their advice. The oldest tomes said a goshawk was the ideal beginners' bird, more recent authors favoured a kestrel, while the most modern said a common buzzard was best. Goshawks are temperamental, difficult and powerful birds, said today's experts, kestrels too small (and anyway useless once trained). Buzzards are easier in temperament and capable of withstanding the inevitable mistakes of a beginner. After an apprenticeship on one of these, one could progress to their more powerful relatives. But who could really want a buzzard? In theory buzzards live on rabbits in the wild, though in practice carrion and small mammals form the bulk of their diet. Almost too slow and inert to catch an adult rabbit, at best it would be trained only to be discarded for a superior bird.

Naturally I wanted a goshawk. I was sure I could overcome its power, that I would not be intimidated by a grip which could drive talons straight through rabbits and hares, but the £1,000 that these powerhouses commanded put them beyond my means. Finally I found the advice I was looking for. One of the contemporary manuals recommended a red tail: the American equivalent of the European buzzard. It was faster and more powerful and could easily take rabbits: large females could even manage hares. Better still, it was within my price range.

Heart in mouth, I ordered a hawk from a Norfolk dealer, the cheque for £425 winging its way to a complete stranger in return for a bird that I had never seen. Indeed, I had only ever once seen the species before, as a ten-year-old shivering in a hall at midnight, my thoughts fixed on an injured kestrel. In return I had a verbal promise that he was feather-perfect and not an imprint.

And now here he was. The van driver grinned at me as I fumbled with pen and receipt, while the box swung wildly on the finger hooked around the binding string as the invisible creature careered around his cramped cell. Built to soar the open skies, he was clearly furious at confinement in a box barely big enough in which to turn.

He had been due at eleven, but as I lay in bed, dozing uneasily and listening to the news, the dogs were restless. Sensing something was going on, I peered out of the window to see a delivery van disgorging its driver. I desperately pulled on my jeans, swearing at the dogs as I tripped over them (luckily it was so cold I was already semi-dressed) and charged downstairs, to find the man delighted by the accuracy of my instructions. It had only taken him an hour to make the trip from Birmingham and now he thought he'd be home early for a long weekend.

'He's very lively,' the driver warned as he clambered back into his cab.

The box bucked and twisted, its irate inmate beside himself with rage. I tried to shake the cobwebs from a brain befuddled by a mere five hours' rest. My heart was pounding as I went inside, just as it had done twenty years before when I had returned with the kestrel knotted in my jersey. I banished the dogs upstairs and took the box down to the cellar. This was the moment of truth. White had fluffed the opening of his basket and seen his bird fly up to a rafter, well out of reach, 'while his master with two pairs of gloves on each hand, cowered near the floor'. Determined to make no similar mistake, I picked a low, windowless room and was, I thought, fully prepared. I carried out the last double and triple-checks: had I remembered everything? It seemed so. Procrastination? Perhaps.

I was still nothing like ready for the volcano that erupted as I ripped open the box. With torch squeezed between arm and ribs, I saw a blur of white as he burst across the darkened room. He landed in the corner and turned, defiant, his beak gaping indignantly, talons clenched tightly into fists of rage. It was my first glimpse of him. He appeared a ghostly cream in the circles of the torch's yellow beam, the pale of his chest flecked with chestnut. His pale eyes were brimming with hatred, his black beak hooked and open, legs splayed out towards me, the feet that are a hawk's main weapons ready to strike.

To say it was difficult to trap him would be an understatement. As I approached he burst past me to the darkened stairs, doubling back to the original corner as I followed him gingerly across the room. Nevertheless, after several attempts, my clumsiness exacerbated by fear of this feathered dynamo, I managed to trap him, tipping my brand new glove over his head to hoodwink him momentarily. Somehow I managed to pin his wings to his sides and attach the jesses. He was not happy, to put it mildly.

6

In this undignified, clumsy manner, the training process had begun and with it the inevitable bate, White's 'headlong dive of rage and terror'. Following him and the countless other falconers who throughout the ages have lifted birds back on to their fists, I raised him back gently on to mine. He bated again. And again. And again. Each time he ended hanging upside down, crucified in gaping indignation, his chest heaving with audible pants. It was clearly safer to move him like this – wings splayed but motionless – rather than risk damage to vital plumage on walls or furniture. I carried him out into the garden and tethered him to his perch, leaving him, his tail splayed out on the grass at the end of his leash, still gasping for breath.

The books say you should let a new hawk settle for a few days after a long journey, but what hope did I have of ignoring him after waiting twenty years? I summoned up enough patience, however, to make a cup of tea, but then couldn't wait for it to cool, and left it half undrunk.

I had to try for a first training session. I went upstairs and drew the curtains in the guest bedroom, leaving just a crack. The semi-darkness should quiet him. Now the question was could I get him to stand on the fist for more than a couple of seconds? It seemed unlikely as I carried him indoors. He would not stay upright, alternately hurling himself off the fist and going rigid, freezing as if suddenly struck with rigor mortis, motionless except for the rapid rise and fall of his chest, his clenched feet incapable of gripping the glove. Again it appeared easiest to carry him inside hanging upside down from the fist.

The manuals say proficient falconers can get new arrivals feeding on the glove within an hour of arrival and even White had managed to persuade Gos to feed after six hours. With experience you could reasonably expect the thing to be flying within a week and hunting within three. I contented myself with trying to persuade my new charge to stand upright, but as he threw himself repeatedly from my fist this looked a hopeless prospect.

After half an hour I knew I was not a proficient falconer.

He had no intention of co-operating with the obviously inexperienced hands dealing with him. The struggle was only worsened when, as I tethered him out in the garden, my neighbour Tony, complete with four Scotties, came past shouting questions. I left the bird, still panting with fury, pegged out on the lawn and retreated inside to make some coffee and a slice of toast.

After a trip to the butcher's to buy a bit of beef shin – the lean but tough cut of meat that is recommended by all the books – I tried once again. This time with more success. He was not prepared to eat, but sat reasonably quietly for an hour or so on my hand, bates punctuating only the first and last few minutes. Incredibly, the dogs both immediately adjusted to his presence, clearing off as if fired by instinct.

I had the bit well between my teeth by now and the second training session in the late afternoon was also a success. My aim should be to get him to feed as soon as possible, the books said. I should not expect too much too fast, but the quicker I could get him to sit quietly and eat, the better falconer I was. As I sat there in the half-darkened room, barely breathing and pretending to look out of the window, he gingerly took a couple of bits of meat from my fingertips and even showed some limited interest in the meat at his feet, though not enough to make him eat. I also managed to feel his 'keel' (breastbone), which seemed sharpish. This, said the books, meant he was not too fat and therefore likely to be fairly amenable.

I also managed to weigh him, but suffered a slight setback when it transpired he outstripped both the metric and imperial sets I had to hand. As a result the two had to be combined and the conversion made with some difficulty (the bird frequently thrashed towards the window). I decided after some thought that metric was the better – after all I am of the right generation – but this, of course, posed some other problems. Try finding a falconry book which uses anything other than pounds and ounces. After much difficulty (and not a little inaccuracy, as he bated every time I placed a weight on the pan) I decided he was, give or take a little, 1,050g (2lbs 5ozs).

Weight is critical in the training of a hawk. The knowledge of this was the edge I had over my mentor, T.H. White. Like generations of falconers before us, we both knew that, unlike a dog, a hawk can only be trained by a series of rewards – in other words food. Even this is not enough, however, as White discovered to his cost. When he could not persuade Gos to eat, he found himself resorting to searching out choicer and choicer morsels, even offending the deepest rules of his upbringing and shooting a partridge out of season. Nevertheless, his progress was painfully slow – but easily explained. Unless the hawk is hungry, the food (and therefore falconer) has no appeal and it will be disobedient. Daily weighing, particularly in the early stages, is now deemed vital to chart the hawk's progress. White was ignorant of this, but I was in possession of the vital key that would unlock the native wildness of my bird. Where he had fluffed and floundered, I would stroll.

For the time being one didn't need to be an expert to see that, at just over a kilogram, he was definitely not too keen to eat off my fist. I decided that I needed to aim for 2lbs – about 900g – a target pinpointed more, I fear, from a touch of pride at having a big hawk rather than based on any scientific calculation.

Still unable to keep my hands off him, I held a final training session, at eight that evening, when he finally ate of his own volition from the fist – another minor triumph. I seemed to be conquering him with little difficulty. Unlike White, who had forced himself and the hawk to stay awake for two days and nights on end, I could now go to bed.

This is where I am now. As I lie here, still too excited to sleep, I have decided to call him Sioux. This is an elaborate joke, which may well prove too clever by half. To begin with, he is by birthright an inhabitant of America, a scrub and forest dweller as free and natural a hunter as any native warrior. Secondly it is a repeat of the old joke we had in my first shared, post-university London household. There all names were transsexual – hence the two female cats were Bob and Bernard and the little bitch puppy became Dill. And then there is the Johnny Cash song, 'A Boy Named Sue' (and the cowboy origin seemed appropriate again). Finally, as I explained my witticism this evening on the phone to one of the few friends who'd encouraged me to go ahead with my dreams, he added a fifth suggestion: 'That's what people will do when he attacks them.'

Saturday 10 October

I WAS AWAKE before dawn, heart still pumping with excitement. I crept across the garden in the gloom before dawn to peer through the glass door of his temporary mews to see him there, a pale form in the shadows. As my eyes became adjusted to the murk, I drank in his every detail.

He seemed to have grown since yesterday. Unused to hawks, I had been surprised by how light he had been when I weighed him, secretly slightly disappointed to find he was a mere two and a quarter pounds. As a human, reared on five-pound chickens and ducks, I had forgotten that these have been bred for the table and that hawks are built for speed not flesh. He stood two foot tall, his back and tail chocolate brown, proving him to be an eyass. (This is an ancient falconry term, meaning originally a chick or hawk taken from the nest, but in today's more regulated world, it usually means captive-bred.) After the moult next spring the tail would turn red, giving him his name.

In contrast his chest was pale cream, almost white, flecked with half a dozen cinnamon feathers. His legs were pale too, dusted with a similar mottling of brown and there, emerging out of the white pantaloons that falconers call his flags, came the legs, yellow and appearing curiously unfinished, covered with coarse scales, roughened, almost splintery, like a crudely cut piece of wood. Nevertheless they were beautiful to me – and so too were his toes, each two inches in length and tipped with a huge claw so black it was blue. These are the tools of his trade, the butcher's knives which make him the most widely-distributed bird of prey in America. Not much larger than his British counterpart, his feet are double the size of his cousin's, making him easily capable of mastering rabbits.

Most impressive of all, however, was his head. Broad and flat-topped, it was big for a hawk. One of my books said this was to hold a brain that was unusually large for a raptor – but that it still weighed less than both eyes. These two baleful yellow discs were certainly big enough, as they stared back unblinkingly at me, still full of resentment. Depending on which expert you believed, these are so sharp they can spot a pigeon moving five miles away or a mouse flitting through grass ten thousand feet below. And finally, jutting out between the eyes was his beak, hooked over in a smooth curve of blue-black that was as silently menacing as a scimitar.

I drank in the sight, enraptured. To me it was a moment of pure poetry. The previous year I had been on a visit to Florence, dutifully doing all the sights, from 'David' to the Duomo and Uffizi. But now, as I stared at him, my bare toes chilled in the dew of an October dawn, arms clasped for warmth across my T-shirt, I knew I had never seen anything so completely perfect. Surely no man-made work of art could ever compare with the pure beauty of a live hawk?

The feeling of awe and respect was clearly not mutual. He saw a half-clad twenty-eight-year-old, spindly white legs covered with goose pimples, hair unkempt and chin unshaven, shivering in the dawn.

His new owner did not inspire confidence. I might consider myself in tune with the countryside, but in honesty, have no reason to flatter myself. Born and bred in Oxford, I have spent my life in built-up areas, most recently six years in London – and four of those in the inner-city squalor of Hackney, surrounded by concrete and brick rather than fields, grass and trees. Certainly I had been immersing myself in a lush Oxfordshire summer, but it was little qualification for the task in hand.

Unlike almost all of my university peers, I had eschewed the call of filthy lucre. While most of them chose the City, accountancy or law for a living, my dreams were instead of job-satisfaction and fame. Initially I had aspirations towards politics, but the experience of canvassing, of knocking on doors and trundling out well-worn arguments to people who were totally uninterested, was disillusioning. Worse were the monthly meetings, the endless squabbling over procedure, dutifully passing motions condemning this or that outrage only to see them – as we all knew they would – immediately ignored and forgotten.

As my hopes of a political career withered when faced with the realities of town hall politics, so had London's appeal wilted. And five years of eating in restaurants, sipping over-priced drinks in wine bars and always talking about (but rarely visiting) the theatre, the place had become threadbare in its appeal. My move to the country was generated by boredom as much as anything. Staring at the hawk I suddenly became almost consumed with panic at the thought that I had acquired this living, breathing, work of art, simply to satisfy a sense of ennui.

What on earth have I got myself into? Red tails can live for thirty years, say the books, and here I am, not knowing what on earth I will be doing in six months – apart from the fact that it almost certainly involves a return to London.

By profession I am a journalist, someone who describes himself, optimistically, as a freelance business writer. If honest, however, I would admit privately to being more of a jobbing scribbler who fell into the subject by chance and knows little or nothing of industry. Worse, I have been lurching from one assignment to another, earning just too little and watching my savings gradually dwindle. During the summer months I was barely treading water financially and this with the advantage of staff holidays leaving magazines with gaps to fill. I think I can cope until Easter – but then my parents will want their cottage back and it looks as if the money will have run out.

Sioux himself was a rash step that I could certainly ill afford – £425 for the bird, £20 for delivery and another £200 on equipment. I comfort myself that it is a one-off expenditure. He represents the annual holiday, second-hand car or new wardrobe that I will forego this year, my little luxury.

Buying him was an impulsive – if also a long-standing – step.

This morning, as I stood there in the chill air staring at him, I suddenly realised that in fact I had no proper experience at all. My clumsy and ultimately disastrous attempt with the kestrel was eighteen years ago and barely counted as a grounding in falconry. I had books certainly, but then so had White and he had made a hash of his attempt. I was churning with a strange mix of elation at the presence of the bird in my shed and terror that I had acted irresponsibly.

As if sensing this, Sioux suddenly threw himself off his perch, flinging his frame away from me towards the corner of the shed and displaying the full extent of his wingspan. Until now I had no idea just how big this was – when he bated off my fist yesterday the proximity and flurry of beating feathers had obscured the length of his reach. Now it was clear: from tip to tip his stretch was a full four feet and each wing almost a foot wide. It was all a little frightening and I retreated inside for a cup of tea and warm clothes.

Refreshed by these, I returned an hour later to try to persuade him to eat off the fist again. This time I had marginally more luck than before and he deigned to stand on the glove as I walked, slower than the guard of honour at a state funeral, to the house. Or at least he remained upright on the fist, his body tensed and leaning forward all the way to the kitchen door. Even my inexperienced eye could see that he was anything but comfortable and wanted to bate. Sure

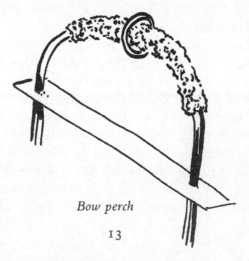

Bow perch

13

enough as the door opened and the darkness of the unlit kitchen loomed up half behind him he threw a tantrum, beating his wings in a desperate bid for freedom. I waited until he had finished the fit before edging him into the room, anxious to avoid any damage to his primaries.

A bird's plumage is vital to its flying ability and most important of all are the biggest feathers on the tail and wings. I was lucky that Sioux arrived in good condition, his plumage a little mute-soiled by his confinement in the travelling box, but otherwise intact. In contrast White's Gos had serious feather damage, with several broken and, almost worse, 'hunger traces' scarring the shafts of undamaged plumage. The last are the minute structural weaknesses caused by stress or poor nutrition. Feathers so damaged will inevitably snap at the mark sooner or later. So far at least, Sioux is unencumbered by any such problems. Although it is possible to repair damage by 'imping' – or grafting another feather on to the broken stump – I am particularly anxious to avoid this. To begin with, because I have only just taken charge of Sioux, I have no feathers saved from the moult with which to make good any problems. More importantly, it would involve having to 'cast' him: getting an assistant to grab him from behind, pinning his wings to his sides, then lowering him, feet first, on to a cushion. This renders him powerless while any necessary repairs are made. Not only do I have no assistant, but the process would be deeply disturbing to both of us, an undignified struggle that would do nothing to improve the bond I am attempting to build.

So I waited patiently until his flapping wings ceased their frantic beating before edging him sideways through the door. Once inside I returned him to the fist and he remained there reluctantly as I walked carefully up the stairs. I had to pause each time he flexed his shoulder muscles and his wings half opened, waiting until he unwound and I could take another few tentative steps.

But the trip was worth it. After two further bates he seemed to notice the lump of meat I was squeezing beneath his toes. He stared suspiciously at the morsel I had arranged temptingly between my thumb and first finger and then slowly, so, so, slowly, he began to lower his head towards it. He was hungry now, not having eaten for two days. The meat was there, red and bloody, easily within reach of his beak. He stretched towards it gingerly, but then I moved slightly. It was inadvertent, but my leg had gone to sleep and I thought it better to move then rather than wait until he was engrossed in the meal.

He bated again, but this time he recovered more rapidly than before and then, suddenly, he was eating, tearing into the meat with his beak, pulling big chunks up quickly. Clearly he didn't trust me and was trying to wolf down as much of the food as possible, while keeping a corner of his wary eye for the slightest movement on my part. In contrast, the books say a relaxed hawk will eat unconcernedly on the fist, bending over the food at complete ease in its owner's presence, interested only in the meat at its feet.

Sioux has a long way to go. After four mouthfuls he lost interest in the fist and returned to standing upright, muscles tensed, those huge yellow eyes glaring at me. Was it my imagination or was there a touch less resentment in his stare? I am not sure, but my spirits were soaring. I returned him gingerly to his perch outside, this time without a bate. Although the whole process had seemed like ten minutes to me, the clock revealed that I had been sitting in the room for an hour and a half.

Sunday 10 October

I SPENT TODAY making him a pen for the garden. I should have built one long since, of course. All the books tell you that this is the first priority, as with all animal arrivals. The creature's comfort must come first and nowhere more so than with an untrained hawk. But I have been too busy to do more than buy the materials. Putting him in the conservatory for safe-keeping, I hammered larch-lap panels together to form three sides of a crude square box and topped it with clear corrugated plastic. The idea is to front the thing with some sort of wire netting, giving him protection from passing dogs – cats are in more danger from him rather than the other way around.

While on the subject of dogs, I have been surprised by the reaction of my two mongrels to the hawk's arrival. Dill in particular is a liability when anywhere near feathers. Broken to cows, horses and sheep, she ignores all blandishments when she gets the scent of a game bird in her nostrils and, full of 'pheasant-induced deafness', chases the stumpy-brown explosion across the stubble, yapping shrilly, to return shame-faced a few minutes later. I was therefore worried about her reaction to the hawk, but in fact both she and her daughter Havoc have been very well-behaved. Clearly there is something about predators which makes them instinctively recognise each other. I suspect it must be the eyes.

Unlike creatures that are used to spending their lives fleeing attack, almost all hunters have eyes positioned in the front of their heads. Their field of vision is comparatively narrow, but designed to pinpoint distances and make out forms. By contrast the hare or rabbit has eyes located further back on its head, giving greater all-round, but less precise, vision. To a rat or mouse it is more important to detect unexpected movement than to identify it. The rabbit hiding in the long grass spots a flicker over its shoulder and is off, scuttling back to the bury. It does this dozens of times a day, taking no chances – and with good cause, when it has so many predators to fear. But cats, dogs and hawks don't live on the edge in this way. Their movements are naturally forward, hunting, stalking and chasing. Psychologists say this explains the human fascination with predators – their faces are cast more in our image than in that of their quarry. Or maybe the dogs just see what I do – the fearless, unblinking stare of a born killer, his yellow eyes boring back into their own inquisitive glances. They leave him alone.

Now that he is settling in, any fears and worries about the wisdom of acquiring him have disappeared. I know now I was right in a decision that has been a serious source of concern ever since I ordered him two months ago. Provided that freelance work continues to arrive, there should never be any real problem. It seems unnecessary to fear that I will lose interest, when my enjoyment of the dogs' company hasn't palled over five years.

I have taken some precautions of course. By buying a red tail I deliberately picked a bird well adapted to the lifestyle of the modern falconer. White opted for the goshawk out of necessity as much as sentiment. The range of species available to him was limited to the old world raptors that had proved their worth over centuries of partnerships with man. In the Thirties the falconer was effectively limited to the goshawk, sparrowhawk, peregrine, merlin and golden eagle. The last is impractical at the best of times and even the ambitious White would have conceded that it was unsuited to a beginner. While merlins and peregrines have a long and honourable history of association with man, they are longwings – falcons – and need large tracts of open country to hunt flying birds.

This left White with the two European hawks, the highly strung diminutive sparrowhawk and the more practical goshawk, known to generations of falconers as the 'cook's bird' for its ability to fill the larder with quarry, ranging from partridges and pheasants to rabbits and hares.

But the range of options open to me was much wider. Since White's time raptors previously considered unworthy of attention are now thought suitable. The common buzzard is generally today's bird for the beginner and more importantly, new species have been imported in large numbers from around the globe. Sakers, lanners and luggers are bigger falcons from the Old World which now compete with the traditional peregrine, and from across the Atlantic have come cooper's hawks, prairie falcons, ferruginous buzzards, harris hawks and red tails.

I had picked the last, in part for its strength and an adaptability which makes it ideally suited to the 'weekend' falconer. Buzzards – or, to give them their latin name, *buteos* – spend a great deal of their time in the wild resting. In practice this means either 'still hunting', perched on top of a suitable vantage point such as a telegraph pole, scanning a large area of land below them, or, more impressively, soaring on thermals. This also involves little or no effort – merely find a thermal, spread your wings and let the rising current of warm air carry you up like an invisible giant lift.

As a result, unlike the falcons which need to be flown every day to get fit, or the highly-strung powerhouse of a true hawk, buzzards fit in well with modern man. They can cope happily with prolonged inactivity, followed by two days' flying. Obviously a bird that lives like this will not be as fit or perform as well as one flown every day, but to treat a buzzard so is in reality merely an extension of what it would do naturally.

By acquiring a red tail I have covered myself for the return to London which seems inevitable, next spring. When my parents reclaim their cottage at Easter, I could, I reasoned when I wrote my cheque, build a big pen in my Islington back garden. Sioux could then spend the four summer months of his moult there, before we returned to Oxfordshire for the winter and his second hunting season.

Monday 11 October

TONY CAME PAST again this morning, with the four Scotties in tow. He was very excited – a kingfisher had turned up on his fence, intending damage to his fish-stocks. The fact that the bird didn't get one made him the more delighted.

I too have been getting a great deal of pleasure out of the creatures I keep spotting around here. For example, I frequently see muntjac, mostly from the car window at night, but Dill coursed one in the field outside the cottage last week and I spotted two more in broad daylight in a nearby wood three days later. The last were a mere twenty yards away, both in resplendent winter coats, one almost black.

Foxes are also in evidence. The hunt killed two cubs in the valley a couple of weeks ago (to the disgust of Tony, who resents the damage the hunt causes and has a sneaking regard for the predators). Havoc actually bumped into one – a vixen on the point of breaking cover in front of me, which the puppy hit on as she nosed her way through a nettle patch. It is hard to say who was more surprised. The dog was taken aback, but not too thrown; while the fox was quicker off the mark, naturally, and hared off in the other direction.

Otherwise, work has been going well and the countryside is wonderful. Seeing the seasons change out here is one of the purest joys of the place. Although the weather has been on the parky side (three days ago was the coldest October night for decades, with a low recorded in a nearby village of -5C), the thought of winter snowfalls inspires me. I have to confess that an important motivating factor in the acquisition of Sioux was the image of myself out in the snow, hawk on fist, that I'd had since childhood. In this dream we silently follow the tracks of a rabbit, padding along after the unsuspecting crea-ture, senses tuned. The rabbit emerges, hopping through virgin powder snow. Breathless, I cast the bird off. There is a flight – quick and to the point. The rabbit jinks and twists, but the hawk follows its every dodge, finally hitting it in a shower of snow as I run in from behind.

It is an unashamedly romantic vision, but one which keeps me happy at night as I huddle under the duvet, listening to the distant screech of an owl.

Friday 23 October

FOR THE LAST couple of weeks life has been very hectic, three days of each being spent in the capital. For two I was working at an ITN office, toiling through nine-hour shifts, writing teletext business news to be flashed up on the tele-vision screens of bored viewers across the country. The third was spent building a pen in my Islington back garden. This is a veritable hawk palace, a huge timber frame covered in welded wire mesh, like a giant, unglazed, greenhouse. The construction dominates the garden – heaven knows what the neighbours think – but it needs to be big if he is to spend the summer in it.

Although of course I would much rather have been out here, at least I can console myself that I managed to persuade my tenant, Vaughan, to cast Sioux, pinning his wings to his sides while I fitted a pair of bells. I fumbled clumsily with the bewits – leather straps – that fix these to his scaly shins, while he gaped indignantly at us both, eyes blinking in surprise and outrage. The result is curiously pleasing, however. His every move is now accompanied by a musical jangling, the same sound which has reassured generations of falconers that their bird is alive and nearby.

The disruption of London visits has badly affected his training schedule however, and his progress has been much slower than I would have liked. Certainly in my dreams I had imagined by now we would have been much further advanced.

Although each manual divides the training process into its own categories, broadly falconry consists of four stages. First comes 'manning', where the feathered dervish is persuaded to sit on the falconer's fist without bating, subsequently being slowly introduced to distractions of increasing scale. In Sioux's case the dogs were the first of these, followed by walks with the bird perched, wild-eyed, but tensed on my fist, and finally, strangers. Once he has accepted all these, the next major stage begins – training.

Here I coax him into first stepping and then jumping on to the fist. When he flies the length of the three-foot leash on to the morsel offered on the proffered glove indoors, the procedure is repeated outside. When this too is achieved, it is time to replace the leash with a *creance*, a light line about fifty yards in length. He is then flown increasing distances to the fist, the falconer safe in the knowledge that should he choose another direction, he can be retrieved. Ideally every flight should be longer than the last, the falconer always edging a step forwards, hopefully never back. It is now that I introduce the lure – an imitation rabbit with meat tied to its 'ears' – dragging it in front of him, hopefully tempting him to chase and 'kill' it. Once he is flying the full length of the creance and chasing the lure, it will be time to fly him free and to start the next stage.

This is the process of getting him fit, without which he

will catch nothing. He is an eyass, the hawk equivalent of a teenager, his muscles still unformed and soft with youth. He was, after all, reared in a small pen in Norfolk, and at least in theory, each training flight should be the furthest he has taken. At first he will be hard pressed to fly a hundred yards without panting and, warn the experts, a two hundred yard flap would be way beyond his powers. In contrast his prey will be lithe and fit, muscles toned by a lifetime in the wild, senses sharpened to a razor's edge. To have a chance of catching anything, he will have to be at the very peak of fitness, as heavy with muscle as possible but without a gram of fat on him.

To achieve this would be to put him in what falconers call *yarak*: an almost untranslatable term meaning in peak hunting condition, raring to go. (Most properly it is used for goshawks which can actually undergo a visible physical change when in the right frame of mind, highly-strung psychopaths that they are.)

To get him fit is merely a matter of exercise – he will require lots of it – and then will come the final stage, the goal which we will both have worked towards from the very beginning – 'entering'. This, in the words of the British Falconers Club, is the very definition of the art: 'Falconry is the sport of taking wild quarry in its natural state and habitat by means of trained hawks. The first duty of all members is to respect and uphold this standard.'

In essence I am to follow the same steps as T. H. White and a millennia of practitioners before him: the principles have remained unchanged since the sport began. The falconer trains his bird by reward alone. He attempts to engineer situations where it, rather than he, initiates the next step – thus the food is held at the hawk's feet when it is hungry, tempting it to lower its head and eat from the fist. The methods that I am to use are the same as those employed by the falconers to the thirteenth-century Emperor Frederick II, the third-century Japanese Empress Jingu, or even Shah Artaxerxes Mnenon, four centuries before Christ.

True, some methods have been dropped, thank God.

White put himself and Gos through the dreadful practice of 'waking' – keeping the bird on the fist for days and nights on end, with neither hawk nor falconer allowed to sleep until a bond has been formed. In contrast Sioux and I are allowed some respite from each other, but the basic theory remains the same.

I have been disconcerted by my slow progress however. According to the experts, buzzards are easy for the first two stages of training, being such bright and easy-going birds that they learn quickly what is expected of them. Manning and training such birds should be a piece of cake, they say: like falling off a log. In contrast, T. H. White's irascible goshawk is one of the most difficult, one day's progress undone the next for no discernible reason, apart from the bird's bloody-mindedness. Once training is complete, the position will be reversed, warn the experts. They say that goshawks have such high energy and adrenalin levels that they seem to be born fit.

It is at this point that the buzzard's temperament begins to work against the falconer. Naturally opportunistic hunters, they are difficult to get really fit and there are no shortcuts, just exercise. And here there will be problems. Because each flight to the fist is rewarded with food and because the bird has a finite appetite, merely flying him in and out of trees will never be enough to get him truly fit. At most the six or seven flights will see him flying a few hundred yards. Instead, probably the best means of getting him to do enough will be to go for walks along mature hedgerows, coaxing the bird to fly from tree to tree, bringing it down to the fist for the occasional reward. That way he has to work far harder for his supper. Once fit, the final stage starts: entering to quarry, attempting to engineer a flight at a wild rabbit.

And that is what is worrying me. Everything seems to be progressing so horribly slowly. I have had Sioux for three weeks, but seem barely to have advanced since his arrival. True, he is coming to the fist all right, flying the three-foot length of his leash readily enough, but I know I should be further advanced in the process. According to the books one should have a buzzard or falcon flying free within a couple of weeks and by now I should be getting him fit, ready to begin hunting. True, allowances are made for beginners like me, but even so, according to the experts, I am making heavy weather, going even more slowly than White before me – and he was making foolish mistakes and working with a goshawk. If it has taken me so long to get a buzzard this far, I am worried that I may never get him ready to hunt, let alone catch anything.

Friday 30 October

IT WAS ONLY by chance that I stumbled across a major cause of my problems: the scales were dirty. With my parents abroad, I 'borrowed' their old-fashioned kitchen scales, removing one pan and bending the supporting spikes upwards. By drilling holes in these, I managed to fix a crude wooden perch on what had been the ingredients side, adjusting the balance to zero with the addition of a few coins beneath it. Unfortunately, however, at some distant point in history, a syrupy solution had been spilled over the machine and as a result both pans were sticking slightly before lifting. Because Sioux was still unhappy about sitting motionless while being weighed, I was guessing his weight at just below that taken to cause the balance to shift, not realising that they were sticking at this juncture. As a result his true weight was considerably heavier than I'd thought. This explains many of my problems; and since sorting it out, his training has taken a sudden lurch forwards. Within a day of the discovery he was jumping on to my fist so quickly that I hadn't the time to shift my glove back to the full extent of the leash. I am beginning to feel more confident about progress and hope that I may have him flying free within the fortnight.

There are also other worries. I would be much happier if he'd show some interest in water and have a bath. The good austringer – keeper of hawks as opposed to falcons – is supposed to provide a bath for his bird every day. They are clean creatures and like to bathe regularly – or at least that's what the books say. So far Sioux has shown not the slightest inclination to tidy himself up. His tail feathers are tipped with the white dust of his mutes, which American falconers coyly describe as 'chalk'. Never mind, no doubt this will come sooner or later.

These are minor quibbles. Much more important is the realisation of how much his presence is altering my life. Until his arrival I was rather smug about my environmentalism. If one allows for a certain degree of conspicuous Western consumption (of unnecessary things like alcohol and meat), I was pretty green: or so I thought. I turned off the hot water in August after realising that I only needed it for washing up (the shower had its own heat supply). Tins, bottles and newspapers were recycled. By cycling to the local shops I created no emissions. In addition, although no gardener, I'd taken to putting all vegetable scraps on the compost heap, wondering at how rapidly the pile built up and how quickly in turn it rotted down. Pile three feet of grass cuttings and potato peelings on top of the mound and within days it had become a mere six inches of well-rotted brown mulch, almost peat-like in consistency.

But now a car has become a necessity. For the last six years I have done without one, cycling everywhere. In London, once one gets over the fear of other traffic, it is quite simply the best way to travel. And when I came out here, so the bike came too. Every day throughout the summer I cycled the two miles into the local town, collecting meat and vegetables.

Then the hawk arrived. Until that point I could cope on trains, buses and tubes with two dogs (just), but add the large and unwieldy box that the hawk travels in and this becomes impossible. The problem is currently being alleviated by the loan of my parents' car, but they return in December and I have the uncomfortable feeling that a major outlay on my first car in six years is looming.

In theory I could stick to the bicycle, but by then the Cotswolds will be gripped by winter and the idea is less than appealing. It seems ironic to be returning to the motorway age because of my fascination with a 4,000 year-old sport.

Saturday 1 November

SOMEONE ONCE TOLD me that T. H. White became interested in falconry because he was a profound pessimist. Like the modern 'survivalists' who build fall-out shelters in their back gardens and spend weekends learning how to snare rabbits and fight off desperate thieves, White was determined to master every skill possible before the apocalypse descended.

If this is true, it is an interesting thought. On the face of it there are much more efficient ways of equipping oneself for disaster. No falconer, however proficient, will ever be able to train a hawk to the same level of killing efficiency as a shotgun or rifle; he would be better advised to practise his marksmanship.

But White was a historian and philosopher. If the end were truly to arrive, proficiency with modern weapons might be a short-term insurance measure; a reliance on the vanished industrialised world. Sooner or later the weapons would seize and the ammunition run out. When that happened where would modern man be? He would have forgotten the skills of the ancients, lost the arts of the bare-handed hunter and forager.

25

No, for White it was not enough to be able to shoot the pheasant or pigeon; he had to be able to catch it using the same methods that have remained largely unchanged since historical records began. Master the goshawk and pass the knowledge on to the next generation. In the event of catastrophe this would be the greatest bequest one could leave.

In the circumstances White was imagining, the durability of the falconer's art, stretching back over four millennia would have been deeply reassuring. Some authorities trace it back to the Hia dynasty in China (which began 2205 BC), others say the falconer in a Babylonian bas-relief dating back to about 1700 BC is the first concrete evidence. Certainly in Britain, from the time it became popular during the Dark Ages until the second half of the seventeenth century, it was one of the most efficient forms of hunting and, apart from netting, the only way to bring down a flying bird.

Since the time of the first surviving written records of the training process (written in Japan in about AD 355), hawking's underlying principle seems to have remained largely unchanged. Where other primitive practices have come to seem uncivilised and barbaric, a kind of social contract with the wild bird, coaxed into accepting the presence of man, has lasted unimpaired into an age of notional equality and mutual respect.

It was the idea of mastering such an ancient sport that reassured White and gave him a sense of security in the uncertain world of the late Thirties. With friends locked in the fight against fascism in Spain and the storm clouds gathering over the rest of Europe, White was unable to face the gloom of his contemporary world. He retreated to rural isolation, with only a hawk for company.

Mulling over this I have gradually realised that in a totally unplanned fashion, I am copying him more slavishly than I'd intended. But for me it is modern, polluted London, and the age of the short-term boom and the long-term recession that seem to demand this unusual cure.

Saturday 8 November

I SPENT THE weekend on my own and was pleasantly surprised at my ability to cope with the isolation. Like most people reared in towns, I crave fellowship – or at least thought I did – perhaps I was scared of finding I didn't like myself, or at best discovering I was boring. But for the past few days at any rate, I have enjoyed life.

A principle achievement was the filling-out of my tax return: or at any rate most of it. As everyone knows, it's a horrible job working everything out – rather grubby somehow, particularly when one has much more pleasant activities to distract oneself with. In London, money seems a nasty necessity, but sitting out in the countryside, looking at the drizzle soaking the field while a pheasant picks disconsolately across the grass, both the city and money seem particularly alien. Out here there somehow seems so much more to life.

Most importantly, the hawk. Now I have mastered the weight problem, training sessions with him are coming on swimmingly, if a tad slowly. The problem is that he is still too 'high', or heavy. He has now dropped to 935g, but unfortunately continues to be disobedient when out-of-doors, surrounded by the distractions of the elements and alien sights and sounds. If I was in any doubt about all this, the proof came when he took off during a training session this morning.

It was my fault for pushing things too far. He was coming the length of the creance promptly, flying low and powerfully to me, rowing through the air with steady strokes of his wings. Excited by what seemed, finally, to be rapid progress, I relied solely on the braking qualities of fifty yards of nylon cord tied to a heavy stick should the worst happen. I was pretty confident nothing would go wrong however: after all, until that point he'd been perfectly behaved, coming quickly to the fist each time I called.

Not this time. Faced with a fifty yard flight, he balked and climbed quickly, rapidly rising above the cottage as his broad wings caught the stiff breeze and flung him towards the village. Faced with visions of a repeat of the incident

Swivel and leash

when, eighteen years before, I'd caught a glimpse of my
kestrel flying off trailing leash and swivel, I swore and charged
after him, praying that the line would snag on something en
route. It did – the hedge beside the next-door neighbour's
garage. His soaring flight ended ignobly as he crashed down
to land in a tangled heap, suspended seven feet above the lane
in an elder bush. I extracted him carefully and took him back,
his feathers ruffled and beak open as he panted from his
exertions.

By this afternoon he was prepared to make another flight
the length of the creance. But in spite of a slight drop in
weight, he was again badly-behaved, refusing to fly promptly
and clearly contemplating another flight into the blue beyond.
Reluctantly I had to abandon the session and put him on short
rations, hoping that by tomorrow he will be obedient enough
to progress sufficiently to be introduced to the rabbit lure.

Sunday 16 November

MY COUSINS CAME over unexpectedly this afternoon,
ostensibly because the sixteen-year-old Thomas wanted to
see the hawk. I suspect the real reason was that Hugh, his
father, visiting the children and his estranged wife, couldn't
think of anything else to do with him and his sister Rosie.

Unfortunately, having just flown Sioux, I couldn't show him flying, but I did pour cups of tea down them, while the hawk sat on Thomas's fist, beautifully behaved for once (Rosie declined the offer).

Hugh, a potter and woodsman by trade, has a particular interest in falconry. A friend of his is pondering the purchase of sixty acres of mixed woodland. Too scrubby and immature to produce much of value, the wood must still pay for itself were she to buy it. His advice is to coppice it, making hurdles from some of the staves, the rest going for firewood. She might also grow hazel-nuts and crocus bulbs. He was interested to see whether or not some form of the sport could be made to pay. I thought yes – if one were to train up four or five Harris hawks and then rent out a day's hawking with them, in the same way that shooting is sold. Hugh, always one with an eye to commercial possibilities, nodded sagely, although it was difficult to tell how convinced he was.

There could be no doubt about Thomas's reaction, however. I dispatched him with a copy of *Cage and Aviary Birds* and a glint in his eye, together with a warning that while it isn't very time-consuming, hawk-keeping is more expensive than one bargains for.

Saturday 21 November

MID-AFTERNOON AND the weather is dull and wet, the drizzle seeping through the air, making it cold as the damp penetrates through to the bone. The conditions are particularly frustrating because I meant to fly Sioux free for the first time today. On Friday he was coming the full length of his creance quickly and he was clearly keen enough. It is now time to screw up my courage and give him his freedom for the first time – potentially risking the loss of everything.

Instead however I have a tremendous sense of anti-climax as I peer out of the window at the fine mist drifting across the fields, soaking everything and ruling flying out of the question. I am sitting here in frustration and have been trying to compensate for the loss of practice by tackling the theory of the appeal of birds of prey with more seriousness. The example of White, important though it is to me personally, hardly accounts for the impact Sioux makes on neighbours, passing strangers and especially children.

Throughout history raptors have been recognised as powerful symbols. The appeal goes far beyond those who fly and own them. The Athenians adopted the little owl as the city's symbol, and this explains that bird's subsequent (but totally undeserved) association with wisdom. And again in ancient history, it is no coincidence that Attila the Hun, the 'Scourge of God', rode into battle with a goshawk on his helmet. As this wild leader of wilder warriors destroyed the world's greatest empire, sweeping in from the Steppes on the fat, slack and decadent Romans, what could better convey his ruthlessness than that most fearsomely efficient and mobile of predators?

Fear, instantly transmitted, is surely the reason that the eagle and falcon are so common on heraldic crests. The Hapsburgs, for example, holy successors to the Roman Empire, took the double-headed eagle as their symbol. In Russia the Romanovs did likewise, and more recently even the world's most modern empire across the Atlantic took the bald eagle as its emblem. Mind you, in this last case, the founding fathers knew little or nothing of falconry and ornithology, choosing one of the least apt of the American continent's indigenous birds of prey. It seemed right for this fledgling country to choose a bird with a hooked beak and six-foot wingspan as its crest, but Benjamin Franklin had well-founded objections. He pointed out that the bald eagle is a carrion-eater, an opportunist that prefers to rob another of its catch rather than hunt for itself. This is the eagle that gorges itself for months on the dying and dead fish of the great Pacific salmon runs. Instead Franklin proposed that the nation should select the turkey as a far more praiseworthy bird.

The power of the image even of a scavenging eagle beats most other birds – not to mention animals – hands down, however laudable their characters. It has a majesty, a dignity striking even to someone who has never seen a hawk in the wild. Similarly, while today's town-dweller may find it difficult to name the visitors to their bird table, almost all of them know what a kestrel looks like. Even this diminutive mouse-killer, fluttering above the motorway verge, catches the modern imagination.

Falconry, together with hare-coursing, is probably the only field sport to have been practised in Britain continuously since Roman times. (Although, come to think of it, the Britons regarded the hare as a holy animal and therefore may well not have hunted it.) Probably the most famous historical reference to the sport comes with *The Boke of Saint Albans* and its well-known list attributing each species of raptor to a particular rank of society. For example an Emperor is assigned the eagle, a king gets a gyr falcon and so on down the list to 'a kestrel for a knave'. But although frequently cited for its reflection of the feudal hierarchy, to a falconer the ranking seems wholly inappropriate. Why assign a baron a common buzzard (which is hard pushed to catch an adult rabbit) while the yeoman gets a goshawk (capable of catching mammals up to the size of a hare and birds as large as a cock pheasant)? And why propose that an Emperor fly a vulture? He would catch more with the knave's kestrel. The erudite White registers this, but he still repeats the list, which seems to have caught the imagination of every falconer to have written a book since. Published half a century after the Black Death had dealt a fatal blow to the feudal system, the book clearly expresses nostalgia for a past order, an idealised age rather than reality.

From the return of the crusaders to the reign of Charles II, falconry and hunting with dogs ruled supreme among the pastimes of the rich. The social cachet of the sport is underlined by the fact that the first European treatise was written by the Holy Roman Emperor, Frederick II, in about 1247. It was the sport of British kings too: Richard the Lionheart took three hundred hawks with him on the crusades and Richard II built the royal mews where falcons were kept from 1377 until 1537 on what is now Trafalgar Square. (Henry VIII was the last British monarch to have been an enthusiastic falconer and it is perhaps no coincidence that it was at about this time that the word 'mews' began to change its meaning from 'hawk house' to 'stables'.)

The traces of the prestige and popularity of falconry are embedded in the language, often in metaphors where the connection is now lost:

> a bate (tantrum); booze (drink, a noun and verb, Dutch in origin, which entered the language via the Lowland trade in falcons); to break into (to tear open the skin of prey, exposing the flesh inside); cadge (the mobile perch on which falcons are carried into the field: traditionally the bearer was paid only by tips, hence its current verbal meaning); cope (to trim a hawk's beak or talons); hoodwink (to blindfold and thus hide distractions from the bird); eyass (a baby hawk or one taken as a baby); eyrie (eagle's nest); to gorge (to stuff the crop, located in the throat – gorge in French – with food); haggard (a hawk trapped in its adult plumage and thus at least one year old); to mantle (spread one's wings over prey, hiding it from potential thieves); mews (hawk's night quarters); musket (the male sparrowhawk); to rouse (to shake the feathers down prior to take-off); to stoop (to plummet downwards on prey); unreclaimed (a hawk that has gone wild); to wait on (to hang in the air high above the falconer, waiting for prey to be flushed); to weather (to sit out in the open air).

Shakespeare's language is particularly thick with imagery derived from hawking. One of the richest and best sustained is Othello's grieving anticipation of the loss of Desdemona:

> If I do prove her haggard
> Though that her jesses were my dear heart-strings,
> I'd whistle her off, and let her down the wind,
> To prey at fortune.
>
> Act III, Scene 3

Even authors as late as Oliver Goldsmith pay the sport tribute. Unless you know that 'a stoop' comes from falconry, then the pun of *She Stoops to Conquer* is missed. And can we trust even the Oxford English Dictionary's lexicographers to pick up every reference? The familiar expression, 'one fell swoop' makes much more sense to the falconer as a 'stoop', conjuring up the image of the steep, lethal fall of a falcon, rather than the tame glide of something like a crow.

Until I was describing the replete Sioux as 'fed up' to Hugh, it had never occurred to me that this phrase also originates with the sport. A well-fed human is neither grumpy nor bored, but the reverse, and full of *bonhomie*. Similarly a trained hawk that has eaten will be calm and good tempered, but the impact of this on its relationship with the falconer is dramatic. A hawk which has been 'fed up' has lost the edge to its appetite. It has no further incentive in pleasing its trainer: lure, prey and fist have no appeal. A 'fed up' hawk wants merely to find a suitable perch where it can digest its meal in peace.

Sunday 22 November

AT LAST THE weather has cleared enough for me to take the huge step of flying Sioux free. In a rare insight into the thoughts of the beginner, one of the text books had warned that this would be a difficult moment, and that most left it far longer than necessary.

This was scant consolation to me, however, as I weighed the bird and went outside. A preliminary flight on the creance went smoothly and then the moment of truth was upon me. Theoretically he should never spot that he was now free, let alone decide to disappear, but theory somehow seemed to count for little as I fumbled to undo the thin cord that was suddenly a vital source of reassurance. I was now a skydiver working without a reserve chute, a stuntman with no crash helmet, a netless tightrope walker.

One of the best defences of falconry against its modern critics is that once trained, the bird only ever returns because it wants to. Once free nothing save education will make it come back. Now the fact that I had spent seven weeks slowly preparing him for this stage rather than the two weeks suggested by the experts disappeared. Instead all I could think of was the wild-feathered bundle that had streaked across the cellar when I had opened the box. As I stared into his eyes while I fumbled with the thin cord, I thought of all those bates, his desperate attempts to put as much distance between the two of us as possible. Had I really remembered everything? What if something appeared now – a tractor, a horse, or a rambler wearing a fluorescent cape? Haunted by my early memories of the kestrel, how shattered I had been by his loss, how I had spent days, weeks, scouring the locality for him, it seemed doubly perilous.

Worse, I was expected for work in London on Tuesday: if he chose to fly free now, I would have at best only just over a day to recapture him – barely twelve hours of daylight!

But there was nothing for it, I couldn't keep him on the creance for ever. The cold and my nervousness made me fumble even more than usual with the cord. Because of the gloved left hand, falconers use a special knot, a form of bowline, which can be tied one-handed. This can be awkward at the best of times, but was now particularly difficult as my fingers, numbed with cold, struggled with the nylon thread. I was terrified that my fear would transfer itself to the bird, that he would sense the visions racing through my mind.

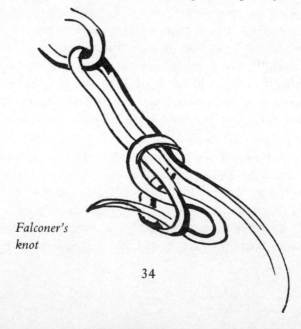

Falconer's knot

With heart in mouth I finally undid the creance and cast him back on to the wall. He alighted easily and turned immediately towards me. Pulse pounding, I shuffled backwards, treading slowly without taking my eyes off him, forcing each foot back. Each fumbling step seemed to take an eternity . . . and then, at twenty yards, it was too much. I lifted my glove and whistled.

He came immediately, without a second thought or so much as a glance over his shoulder. I cast him off with more confidence for a second flight – and then again for a third. Not so much as a hiccup marred the session and it was with an almost delirious end-of-term feeling that I took him back to his perch after half-a-dozen flights.

We are finally getting somewhere!

Sunday 29 November

UNTIL NOW, if I have been worried by Sioux, it has been a minor problem (such as his continued indifference to taking a bath), or impatience at our slow progress, owing to my inexperience. Now the difficulty which is beginning to cause more than a stirring of uncertainty is the fact that he is becoming increasingly vocal – decidedly so. At first I was pleased by the way in which he had 'cheeped' whenever I went to take him up for a training session. Pleasure faded when, during the course of last week, the greeting began to change to a shrill scream. This is deeply worrying. I am beginning to suspect he may be an 'imprint' – a heinous fault, according to experts.

Imprinting occurs when birds are bred in captivity and is a result of the breeder being either careless or greedy during the first few weeks of a chick's life. If the eyass sees a human providing food and begins to associate humans with its meal ticket, a Pavlovian reflex can develop. The same reaction is of course also triggered by its parents and basically means 'Feed me now!'

In the wild this disappears naturally, as the bird begins to hunt for itself. If it ever does reappear, it is in a mild form during the breeding season when the female calls to her mate to pass over food. The problem for the falconer is that the captive hawk needs to be kept hungry, and will thus scream every time it sees its owner. This is, to put it mildly, undesirable. Not only is it irritating, but in bad cases it can produce a very aggressive creature which screams incessantly.

In a big hawk – such as Sioux – imprinting can be positively dangerous. In contrast to an adult bird captured from the wild, which never loses its innate respect for humans, the imprinted eyass becomes fixated on its owner and loses all fear. As a result it can attack in a jealous rage. To make matters worse for me, I have a vague hankering one day to breed birds of my own, and an imprint will never be able to reproduce naturally.

So it was with a sense of foreboding that I heard his greeting on Thursday morning. Suddenly, after weeks of silence, he now screeches whenever he sees me. And each time he opens his beak the word 'imprint' screams at me too. It appears that, as I have brought down his weight, the imprinting, buried deep down in his primaeval feeding instincts, has come to the surface.

But if the thought of the hawk being an imprint is worrying and his scream unpleasant, I would far rather spend time with him out here than in the *Oracle* office in London. At first the money was welcome, being just enough to tide me over as I waited for 'real' work – writing features at home in the Oxfordshire countryside. In addition, I was frightened of losing the benefits of urban life, the company and work contacts. Thus when offered the chance of shifts, I welcomed the idea. Spending part of the week in the city seemed the perfect way of balancing my life. Five days of peace and tranquillity, two days of hectic work and socialising.

It hasn't worked that way. To begin with I've begun to loathe the drive into London. Every time I shoot along the raised motorway into the metropolis, the silhouette of the City looms up like the cinematic nightmares created in films like *Brazil* or *Bladerunner*. Each time this vision appears, the dark skyscrapers etched against the sky seem to be an ever darker shade of grey and I get a choking feeling. It is increasingly difficult to make that drive without the image of the fog in *Bleak House* swirling into my mind's eye – a dank clamminess which snakes through my body, snuggling into the innermost soul. By the time I reach Paddington, I am invariably thoroughly depressed.

Worse, work has lost most of its novelty and become positively disagreeable. As the seconds tick away towards the end of the day, the old hands are getting short-tempered. I'm beginning to wonder why I am working my arse off in London, being yelled at by people I don't like, without too much of a cash flow in return.

Tuesday 1 December

A RURAL WINTER has now brought other problems – a mouse explosion. I returned last week to find signs of them in the kitchen. This happens every year and I paid little attention. I merely set a couple of catch-'em-alive traps, anxious not to kill needlessly. Unfortunately, however, these are inefficient, made for squeamish townsfolk faced with one errant visitor from outdoors. They need time to work and are not the sort of thing with which to face a seemingly endless invasion of the creatures.

During the weekend the number of sightings assumed alarming proportions. I caught one in a humane trap, but it was soon clear that it was impossible to stand in the room for more than five minutes without seeing little brown flickers out of the corner of one's eye. When a guest, Rosie, picked up a tea towel and two very healthy mice fell out, there was nothing for it.

Last night I pulled out the old 'Little Nipper' traps, bought for 10p each many years ago and, with a little fine tuning with the pliers, set them on hair triggers in cardboard boxes on the kitchen floor (to keep them away from the dogs' noses). I then went out for a birthday drink with a friend near Oxford, returning to find both had gone off – but were without occupants. Re-tuning them again to an even more sensitive touch, I reset them at midnight and sat down with a mug of tea to listen to the news. By the time it had finished, two mice had bitten the dust by the freezer. By this morning another three were added to the total, with just one lucky individual sitting washing itself on the windowsill by the taps, encased in the brown plastic box.

I released it and have put the others in the freezer, consoling myself with the fact that at least I needn't feel any qualms about killing with the hawk sitting outside. They are excellent food for trips to London, one per day being the right daily ration for a Sioux who still needs to be brought down slightly in weight. Better still, they are full of vitamins, roughage and trace elements. It reminds me of that comment a fellow don had made about the falconer who helped me with the kestrel: 'He's the only person I know who actually encourages mice in his barns.'

In the interim all is going reasonably well with Sioux. He is now flying free all the time, although it has to be said that he is far from fit and we are still a long way from being ready to hunt. But for the time being, seeing him fly is enough – just to watch him come in hard and fast, rowing himself into the fist, his eyes burning holes in my glove. I continue to be surprised, however, at how low he flies – a mere six inches above the ground, so close that even with shallow wing-strokes, the tips of his four-foot wingspan brush the grass. Then, as he arrives at the last few feet, he suddenly shoots up on to the fist, landing much more lightly than you expect. Although his training needs a lot more work, it seems as if the worst is now over and that I can soon start exercising him along the local hedgerows. With luck, I hope to have him really fit and hunting by Christmas.

As I wait to reach this point, I have been walking and driving around the area with newly-peeled eyes, senses tuned for potential quarry. Somehow, merely being in the presence of Sioux is turning me into a raptor myself. I have found that I can type and scour the field behind the computer out of the corner of my eye at the same time. When driving, particularly at night, my eyes are on the verge, hunting like a kestrel or barn owl for movement. It is in this way that I caught a glimpse of a weasel last week – my first for years. In addition I keep seeing foxes, muntjac and partridges. The last in particular are encouraging, not because Sioux would catch them (red tails are far too slow for that), but because, living off small insects and grubs, their numbers are an indicator of the general health of the lowest levels of the food chain and hence of elements further up. The same goes for the weasel.

More significant was yesterday's glimpse of a merlin just above the village. These small falcons are really birds of the heath and moor, but are agile enough to exist in enclosed countryside. They are certainly found in Oxfordshire, but in places like Otmoor and the Downs. I have only ever glimpsed one once – and that was in the Cambrian Mountains. Thus the sight of one flying fast towards a local plantation was something to make the heart sing.

Thoughts of hawks are now increasingly filling my thoughts. With Christmas coming, I spend increasing amounts of time surveying falconry catalogues. In particular I have been considering a hood, which is pointless for training Sioux, but is the first germ of a new idea.

Which reminds me, the lack of a hood so far has puzzled many friends. To most people, falconry invariably involves hooded birds sitting hunched on aristocratic fists. Certainly in its purest sense this is true. Hoods are a vital part of training

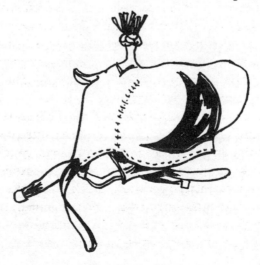

falcons, as opposed to hawks and buzzards. They quieten the bird, removing the temptation of distant quarry. With a falcon this is essential. Long distance experts among raptors, these can chase birds that are too far away for them to have a hope of a kill and then find themselves lost. In addition, groups of falcons are frequently flown in the same place, one after the other. It is important to keep those that are grounded from becoming jealous of their airborne colleagues.

But a hood is undesirable for a hawk or buzzard. For one thing these are short-distance specialists, and the latter in particular are unlikely to fling themselves after a distant speck of disappearing fauna. For another, not being able to see what is going on also means that the bird is not being 'manned' – getting used to the sights and sounds that are the inevitable part of captive life.

No, I want a hood merely to practise putting the thing on my bird. I can't help dreaming that perhaps one day circumstances will change to allow me to progress to a falcon. Clearly this is a thought which will have to remain a pipe dream for the foreseeable future. To own such a creature without flying it every day would be an abomination and with my return to London at Easter, clearly impossible.

Monday 7 December

THE TRAINING CONTINUES at a steady pace, but has been further complicated by Sioux developing a second vice, less annoying than the screaming, but still something I would prefer to do without. He is increasingly 'sticky-footed'. In practice this is exactly what it sounds like – most of the time the bird appears to be stuck to the glove. The problem is that he is so highly strung that his foot muscles tighten, locking his feet in a vice-like grip to whatever he happens to be sitting on. Should he then decide, of his own volition, to leave the fist for a convenient tree he is brought up short immediately, his feet still locked to the leather. And there he hangs, suspended upside-down from the glove, his beak gaping wide at the indignity of it all, but still incapable of releasing himself. Lower him gently to the ground and he merely lies there, still locked to my hand. The more he wants to part company, the more he resents the enforced imprisonment, and the tighter his grip becomes. There is no alternative but to prize his claws apart or to grip his ankle tightly with the right hand and pull the glove slowly out of his hold. According to the books almost any hawk can be sticky-footed, but, they note ominously, red tails are particularly prone to this vice – in one expert's view yet another reason for the beginner to avoid the species.

Apparently most birds grow out of the habit as they mature, but in the short term it is irritating. The slightest upset, the merest heightening of his adrenalin (with a partially-manned hawk, it doesn't take much to raise this) and his feet clench tight, bolting us together. He is still too unfit to be ready to tackle rabbits, but unless he calms down soon, it is clearly going to be a problem for the future.

Mind you, as with almost everything that he does, the mere issue has prompted me into one of my rambling trains of thought that form a large part of his appeal.

If it is a fault common to eyass red tails, perhaps the characteristic has a function? The books give no hint of what this might be, but having had ample opportunity to see it at first hand, so to speak, I have developed my own theory. Perhaps, as an eyass lacking expertise, there is much to be said for a vice-like grip which is almost impossible to dislodge? As I imagine it, the bird is sitting on a telephone pole, surveying the undergrowth below. It sees a rabbit under a bush and swoops down on the thing, but at the last moment the intended quarry sees its attacker and turns tail. Instead of landing on the head and ribcage (as most raptors do by instinct) it connects with only one foot and that is on the creature's hindquarters. A tussle ensues with the bird thrown around like a cowboy on a bronco as it desperately tries to grab the unfortunate beast with the other foot. Provided the animal is not too big and the hunter succeeds in catching it with both feet, there is a good chance of a kill. Were they not locked together, it would be kicked off, leaving the hawk looking bruised and foolish in the dust.

Later on, when the red tail is a more proficient killer, it should lose this involuntary grip. Once it has proved that it can feed itself, the balance changes and being incapable of letting go is a bigger disadvantage than benefit. Again in my mind's eye I picture a red tail seeing something stir in the scrub below. As an opportunistic hunter, secure in its own killing ability, it drops on the flash of brown and grey fur, only to discover it has attacked a big hare, fox or worse, a coyote. A tussle with any of these is at best going to be unsuccessful (with the serious risk of damage to vital plumage), and at worst could prove fatal. Under these conditions the buzzard does well to let go and beat the quickest retreat possible.

Tuesday 8 December

MY RESPECT FOR Sioux took a great leap forward at the weekend thanks to a foolish mistake which led to my first serious 'footing'. Of course I'd been caught by his claws lashing out before, but this was the first time that he had got me properly. I was about to fly him and had just removed his slitted mews jesses. Not concentrating, I put the discarded leather strips into my hunting vest – into the pocket immediately above the one I use as a food store. As I pulled out my hand, a flash of orange and pink caught my eye. It was a jay flitting past the window. My attention wandered for a moment as my right hand strayed towards his leg. I began to wonder why it is that their nests are so difficult to find – in marked contrast to the nests of their cousins the crows, jackdaws and magpies.

It was only a momentary lapse of concentration, but I paid for it. As I looked back towards Sioux, his foot lashed out. To describe the next moment as slow motion would be misleading. It was a mixture. My reactions were slow, his lightening quick. I barely saw his leg as it fired out, but the pain seemed to follow an age later. I looked on as his claws sank into my unprotected right hand. I should perhaps say that these are now well over an inch in length, and because he has been perching on grass and feeding off soft meat, they have had nothing to file them down and are needle sharp.

As the black curves of nail disappeared easily into the ball of my thumb, the pain was delayed. The first sensation was of pressure – a bone-crunching vice of a grip, and then the sharp pain of punctured flesh. Still in slow motion, the pink of blood marked out the entry points, as if underlining the pain, and drops swelled beneath the blue-black of the nails. It trickled slowly down my hand.

This presented me with several problems. The grip of a red tail is more than averagely powerful, as the words of a Canadian falconer testify:

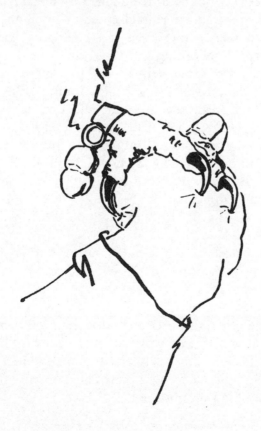

Red tails take perhaps the most tenacious and concentrated grip of their prey of any raptor other than a golden eagle. They kill entirely by the numbing compression of the grip and by talon penetration, sitting back on the spread tail with spread wings and raised head and crest, awaiting the total cessation of breath and movement.*

As I stood there in the kitchen, blood dripping slowly down my hand to spot on to my stained and soiled leather work boots, I could testify to the accuracy of Beebe's descriptive powers. But I had a more immediate problem than wondering about the technical details of Sioux's killing technique. I was on my own in the house, held by a sticky-footed hawk, rage in his heart. There was no one to release me from his grip and I was as effectively bound as if pinioned by metal handcuffs – and in considerably more pain. I couldn't reach any food to tempt him to release me; even if I could, he was almost certainly incapable of letting go.

Worse still, any movement on my part merely produced an increase in the pressure. The programming of his instincts over generations meant that any movement on my part signified life to be squeezed out of prey. As the blood tick-tacked on to my boot, dull plops beating with mortality, merely drawing breath on my part was enough to produce agonising increases in the pain. Perhaps fortunately, his claws were prevented from going too far by a solid that even he could not penetrate. But as I felt them grate on the bone, this was little consolation.

There was nothing for it but to wait. And so we stood there, looking each other in the eye. Mine were watering, while his yellow discs were flared with indignation. His neck feathers were up and his chest was heaving with the exertion of keeping the grip tight. If Beebe's description was inaccurate in any way, it was that he was not sitting back on his spread tail – but then he couldn't while standing straddled between the two hands. The silence was punctuated only by the steady noisy drip of blood on my boot.

* Frank Beebe, *The Compleat Falconer*, Hancock House, 1992

44

After ten minutes it became obvious that this could be a lengthy process. If anything his hold was tighter than ever and the pain more unbearable. There was nothing for it, I decided, but to pull myself free. Anxious to save him from any possible damage, I managed to manoeuvre my gloved left hand across to his left leg which was fastened to my right hand and got a finger and thumb on his ankle. I didn't want to put too much pressure on his hips, and by holding his leg firmly with my fingers, I calculated I could drag my hand away without hurting him.

I won't describe the next five minutes save to say that the tears were streaming down my face as I ploughed his claws through my flesh, four tracks left gouged in the flesh, each welling with blood. At last it was done and he was back with both feet on the glove. As may perhaps be imagined, my enthusiasm for flying him had abated somewhat. Of course he still had to be tended to and the first priority was to go slowly back to the pocket, to withdraw the jesses and to return my dripping hand to within range of his foot again. He feinted at it, claws still wet. While I fiddled with the jesses, he pecked at the bloody gouges – more pain but nothing compared to the past few minutes. Nevertheless I managed to get the jesses on relatively quickly and returned him to his perch in the garden, tossing him a chick as I left.

And all the time I could show no pain, no annoyance and still less resentment at my torturer. As I drove twenty miles to the nearest out-patients' department, I pondered the irony of all this. Here is one of the most aggressive and powerful of birds, one which hunts with lightning reactions, an instinctive hunter, and yet the training process requires me to be the antithesis of his character. If his reactions are to snatch, so mine must be smooth and easy. Power is countered with gentleness, tantrum greeted with patience, pain with kindness and a wound with a reward of food.

In spite of all this, I have no regrets about acquiring him. Not a bit of it. In fact, as the six stitches went in, I was trying to work out whether I would be back in time to fly him before dusk. If so, would he be calm enough or would he still be in a fury which would make the exercise counter-productive? Few people can understand this and certainly the houseman patching me up showed little comprehension. Why own such a treacherous beast? Why risk tetanus and septi-caemia, to say nothing of the pain and blood-loss? What could possibly make it worthwhile?

As I drove back, I just smiled at the thought of his bewil-derment. And the smile broadened when I got back to the cottage and saw the hawk on his perch, crest raised while a scream, mercifully inaudible above the noise of the car radio, came spitting out of his beak.

Tuesday 15 December

I AM FREEZING – chilled to the bone. The reason? Winter is definitely here and thanks to Sioux I have just spent three hours standing largely motionless below local trees, whistling in vain for him to descend. The problem came when I decided to fly him this afternoon, in spite of his weight being a little higher than I might have wished.

I ignored the danger signs when he refused to come twenty yards to the fist, but instead stood there staring around him, blind to my proffered glove. He clearly had little interest in the garnish of rabbit thigh and eventually only deigned to fly to me when I halved the distance between us. It should have been a warning – indeed I knew I was foolish to continue – but I have to go to London tomorrow for work. I was desperate to get in what would be our last outdoor training session before the weekend and took the gamble, buoyed up by increasing confidence in the bonds that I can feel being built between us.

I walked on, hawk perched on my glove, pondering the wisdom of my decision. I was beginning to change my mind as I contemplated the risks. I decided to give him one more test flight and cast him off towards the fence guarding a little spinney of half-grown trees in the middle of the field.

Sioux flapped off slowly, clearly lacking motivation. As he reached the halfway point he changed his mind. The direction of his laboured flight swung left and he pitched into a large ash, ten feet or so above the ground. I cursed him, realising that this would have to be his last flight. He may only have been flying free for three weeks, but already I can tell his mood from his wingbeats. As he landed in the tree I knew I had made a mistake.

Little did I guess how unpleasant this lesson would prove to be. I stood beneath him brandishing my glove and whistling – or rather I attempted to whistle, but the cold meant that little emanated from my pursed lips other than something between a puff and a raspberry. It held little appeal for the bird above my head. He merely stared across the field, his head turning as he followed the flight of a distant pigeon, took in a flock of sheep quietly grazing on the other side of the valley and heard the sound of a chainsaw starting up somewhere in the village. He was ominously quiet too – a lack of sound which shows that food is not the first thing on his mind.

I stood there beneath him, my boots brushing the frost off the grass, fist held above my head and waited . . . and waited . . . and waited while a deep red sun slid slowly across a clear sky behind me. I cursed myself again for my impatience, stamping my feet on the hardened ground to keep the blood flowing through my toes.

Eventually – I suppose it must have been an hour or so later – I thought I detected a change of mood on his part. His head tipped forward and he stared intently at the meat. He shuffled along the branch and peered down at my fist and I was relieved to hear his screams becoming more frequent.

But then, just as he leaned so far forward that it seemed impossible that he could remain on the branch, there was a noise in the lane. A couple with their baby and dog were walking along the track. They were talking quietly. The murmurs destroyed Sioux's mood totally. Instead of tumbling down on to my glove, he flung himself sideways, flapping away towards the village.

Swearing loudly, I ran after him, pounding through the grass, the cold air chilling my lungs until they ached. I am unfit and the two hundred yard sprint left me with a stitch. Fortunately he didn't go too far, pitching into a sycamore near my neighbour's. He was perched a good forty feet above the ground in a tree which was obviously unclimbable.

I was back at square one. He landed around two-thirty and, as the sun set an hour-and-a-half later, he was still there with no sign of any inclination to come down. Instead he sat there, staring around him. In particular he seemed intrigued by my neighbour, Tony, who was gardening below. The presence of the man only added to my frustration: not only did he deter the hawk from the lure of the rabbit, but he was witness to my ineptitude as a falconer. (There was no hope of the two of us escaping his notice with Sioux's screeches punctuating the clear afternoon air.)

As the sun slid below the horizon and it became increasingly difficult to see him, I had to concede defeat. There was nothing for it but to leave him there, hoping that at least the chill of a night spent exposed to the elements would bring his weight down enough to instil obedience. I could only pray it would: I think it unlikely that my boss at *Oracle* would understand the excuse of having to stand in the open, for days if necessary, waiting on the whims of a hawk.

I consoled myself that at least Sioux would be going nowhere in the dark and the tree was little more than a hundred yards from the cottage door. In addition, with the longest night of the year only a week away, dawn would be just before eight and so an early start would not be called for.

I sighed and turned on my heel, heading for the house. My shoulders were sloped with disappointment, my back ached with the effort of holding the glove up and my lips were chapped badly – I had licked them almost continuously in an effort to coax out sound.

And as I turned, the note of his cries changed. I could hardly believe it: he was about to come down! Turning back towards him, I thrust up the glove, straining my eyes to see him in the gloom. There he was, his wings half-folded as he dropped steeply down on my glove, a white form framed against a dark deep blue sky.

MY PARENTS HAVE now got back from America to mixed reactions on my part. On the one hand I am a loving son and glad of the opportunity to talk and eat with them, but on the other it presents something of a dark cloud on the horizon. The cottage in winter is too cold and damp for their taste, but this is bound to change in the spring when they will want it back, exiling me to London for the summer – what a horrible thought! At least it inspires me to redouble my efforts on the hawk's training – a sort of hourglass ticking away in the background, measuring out the flying time I have got left.

But their presence has also given me fresh insights into the bird. My father is fascinated by – although wary of – the creature and through talking to him I have had the chance to consider my relationship with Sioux. For example, last week I mentioned how my obsession was growing: 'I have been taken over and am now owned by that bird,' I said in passing.

'What do you mean, owned?' He exclaimed. 'He's your slave!'

How little most people understand falconry – even my own father. In spite of all the boring monologues he's had to listen to, regardless of seeing Sioux in the flesh and watching him fly, Dad thinks that ours is a conventional animal/human relationship. It is of course nothing of the kind.

Certainly at the outset the hawk might be a captive, held against its will by leather, swivel and leash, but it is a prisoner of war, a hostage, not a slave. Once flying free, he is exactly that – free. He can choose to return, or he may disappear.

'But you've trained him to do that,' remonstrated Dad. 'He's not acting naturally, but artificially, conditioned by you.'

Well, certainly I have trained him. If you were to put meat on your fist or swing a lure, you'd have to wait a very long time indeed before a wild goshawk or peregrine came down to it. And of course the same is true of persuading a wolf to pull a sled, or a wild horse to run towards the bridle. All animals need to be trained to some extent, even if only to accept man as a friend and not an enemy. Given that, relationships between man and beast differ as widely as the species involved. A horse or a dog forms an active bond with its master. It can be trained both by reward and punishment and will come rapidly merely on command, expecting neither reward nor reprimand. *That* is the master/slave relationship. With cats it is the reverse. Pretty much untrainable, they hang around human company merely because it suits them and leave happily when a better deal comes along, be it nicer food, a warmer house or more regular meals. The owner is the slave, the cat the master.

With a hawk it is different yet again. Training is best summarised as the attempt to persuade the hawk that being in human company is preferable to life on its own. Make a mistake and the hawk will choose to go solo. If this happens, you are unlikely to see it again. No punishment can be involved in the process. Such visible animosity that exists is all one-way – the bird hates its handler. The falconer puts his new bird on his fist: it bates. He lifts it gently back on: another bate. He puts it patiently back, and tries to distract its attention by squeezing its toes between a slab of bloody steak: it may deign to eat – or more probably will bate again. Were it a dog, by this stage the hand, the whip or at the very least, the voice would have been raised.

Master and slave? To hunt with a hawk is to make it self-sufficient. The better it gets at killing, the more able it is to fend for itself and the less it needs to return to its keeper. What Louisiana plantation owner ever gave his slaves return tickets to the destination of their choice? That is what the hawk owner does every time he casts off his bird. I would freely admit that the two dogs look at me as their lord, master and God, but to suggest that Sioux returns because he knows I am boss is ridiculous. Only social animals can be trained to be slaves: creatures of the herd, pack or family. Hawks are loners and so cannot be awed by displays of superior strength.

Wednesday 6 January

THE FIRST ACT of the New Year was the acquisition of a new car. I bought it at an auction, forking out a great deal less than I'd budgeted for. It might be rusty, but it is big enough for my menagerie and seems mechanically sound. It is strange to have a car of my own after six years of coping with just a bicycle.

The new possession has prompted a wave of nostalgia for those heady days after I passed my test. I find myself making excuses to go for a drive. Today, for example, I went to Evesham – a pleasant chug across the Cotswolds using the back roads. This should have taken three-quarters-of-an-hour according to the map, but actually took twice that. Admittedly this was due in part to getting slightly lost, but was mainly because I got held up by a fox hunt (not by the hounds and horses, but by the lane-crawling 'townie' followers, in their pristine Escorts and Cavaliers). This is the second time in a week or so that I've run into the hunt – figuratively rather than literally – and it has made me think.

As a starting-point, I can see no problem with killing foxes. Around here they are a considerable pest and man is the only limit on their numbers. There used to be half-a-dozen small flocks of poultry in the village, but now there is just one. It belongs to the only person rich enough to afford the elaborate fencing and still frequent losses. Gassing, shooting and poisoning are alternative means of control but all have drawbacks. The first and last are both unpleasant and indiscriminate – there is no way of telling how many of what species one is killing – and shooting, contrary to the visions portrayed on the screen where victims drop dead or at worst expire quickly, is far from a certain death. Wounded foxes frequently die of gangrene and lead-poisoning weeks later.

In contrast, fox hunting is not only clear-cut, with the fox either dead or alive after a chase that is rarely longer than a few minutes, but it is also fairly ineffective, with the creature escaping far more frequently than not.

This might seem like a contradiction. Either one wants to

control foxes or not, you may say. Well, yes, but there is control and control. It is probably true to say that if it weren't for hunting there would be no foxes and precious little woodland in southern England. They would have gone the way of every other significant predator, shot, trapped and poisoned out of existence. The little copses that dot the landscape would have gone the way of the great forests that once cloaked the entire country. It was hunting-mad squires who insisted that foxes were preserved by their keepers and refused agents permission to plough up the last of the woods for the sake of giving foxes somewhere to breed.

It is still true to a certain extent. Our local hunt pays secret bounties to farmers on whose land foxes are found – and I know of at least one who gets backhanders for feeding his. As a result there are probably more foxes around here than there would be but for the hunt. The depletions of local poultry are the inevitable consequences of a policy of toleration.

Nonetheless, for all this defence of hunting, personally I find it distasteful. I don't believe one commonly cited argument: that it is indefensible for the participants to enjoy the killing. If it is necessary for some foxes to die, the fact that the killers enjoy themselves is neither here nor there. No, hunting displeases me because of its formality and upper class trappings. (In spite of what proponents tell you, merely to ride to hounds costs thousands of pounds each year in horse maintenance, clothing and hunt fees, while to be a master costs obscene sums annually.)

To me, any form of hunting animals is a way of getting close to nature first and foremost, and of achieving a purpose – such as eating – second. I have rarely killed anything, but over the years I must have stalked thousands of creatures and thus found myself far more in tune with what is going on. In the same way the hawk means I keep my eyes open. I am reminded of Teddy Roosevelt's comment that he used to study grizzlies in order to hunt them, but later hunted bears in order to study them. I find it hard to see how you can call a hunt getting close to nature. Galloping in a crowd across fields, following a pack of ungainly hounds and a red-coated (sorry, *pink-coated*) man blowing an out-of-tune horn is not the best way to see wildlife, whatever proponents might say.

But I digress: the purpose of my drive to Evesham was to buy deep-frozen day-old chicks. I know that to most people this may seem vaguely distasteful, but to the hawk-keeper the availability of unwanted chicks is a blessing. They contain the essential vitamins and roughage that do a hawk all manner of good; a couple each day will keep Sioux on his toes and in the peak of health.

I was delighted to find a supply after three months of trouble and expense feeding him beef shin. There was, however, a slight drawback. They are only sold by the two hundred. Now, had I had a straightforward journey, wasting just forty-five minutes rather than an hour-and-a-half, perhaps I might have paused to think that a couple of hundred chicks at two a day feeds a hawk for over three months. But, feeling slightly flustered, I didn't think and ordered two boxes instead. Not only will this keep Sioux going the best part of seven months, but they will also take up considerable space in the freezer, virtually all of it to be precise.

Also, now that the freezer is chock-a-block with frozen yellow corpses, another problem occurs to me. I am far from sure that Mum and Dad will share my initial delight. For not only do they obstruct things in the freezer beloved of parents, such as convenience foods, but I suspect they might run counter to their sense of the aesthetic. After all, the conventional view of a fluffy yellow chick is that it is best looking sweet and pecking around behind its mother in some bucolic farmyard, or at the very least gracing an Easter card. At any rate, popular opinion holds that it is nicest alive.

On the journey home I rehearsed my explanation. To get an egg or a pint of milk you need a hen or a cow. To get one of these in turn, two eggs or calves have to hatch or be born, because on average one will be male and one female. The hen or cow will go on to great egg- or milk-producing feats, but the little cock or bull will never – no matter how hard he tries – produce eggs or milk. What should the farmer do? See his fields gradually fill up with useless bovine mouths, stripping the grass from the land? Feed an ever-burgeoning flock of cocks (who will, for social reasons, be perpetually locked in fights with each other)? Not at all. In the case of bullocks they will end up in some sort of pie, in the case of an egg-laying poultry breed, it will be sexed at one day old and then half will be gassed. Given he's a carnivore, my hawk might as well eat chicks as see them thrown on the compost heap.

Thursday 7 January

FINALLY SIOUX HAS begun to fly well (not before time). His progress suddenly seems to be coming on in leaps and bounds. A week ago he was flying slowly to and from the fist, screaming all the time. Now he is doing exactly the same, only more quickly. To an outsider there is virtually no change, but the difference has made me almost ecstatic. In just a few days we have taken a huge step forward, he is beginning to approach fitness and is now almost ready to enter.

The reasons for the improvement are complex – and I am not even sure I know the exact causes. I think that the main problem has been fluctuating weight and a lack of confidence on both our parts, but the new diet also seems significant.

Before, when he was being fed on lumps of meat, I would give him a couple of mouthfuls before quietly removing the lump from between his feet. This accounted for much of his 'footing': he associated my left hand with food, but resented my right as a rival which took it away. Now, however, I am feeding him on chicks which I dismember beforehand. Because he is now getting just a leg, say, there is no need to take anything from him; hence no sense of rivalry and less aggression. Another benefit is that it is much easier to judge the quantities of food he is getting. His weight remains stable on one whole chick plus the heads and legs of two others (a side advantage of this is that at a rate of three chicks a day I will have an empty freezer by June).

The prompt for this outburst of delight is that we've just had easily the best training session I've had since I began to fly him free. His progress over the past few days was sufficiently good for me to decide this morning to try to build up muscles with some training 'walks'.

It is impossible to describe how exhilarating it is to see him 'following on'. Now, after all these weeks, we have built up enough of a bond for him not only to come when I call him to the fist, but to want to keep me in sight. This morning I walked along a couple of hedgerows, occasionally holding up my glove adorned with a choice tit-bit. He followed, slowly and clumsily admittedly, but he definitely followed.

Perhaps because the surroundings were new to him, he was comparatively quiet too, his mewing scream a little less grating than normal. He flew once or twice from tall trees before, excitingly, he used a slight breeze to describe a broad arc across the field. His hunting instinct is obviously beginning to emerge. On the most spectacular flight, he flew a good hundred and fifty yards away from me, before turning into the wind and quartering the field, hanging in the breeze for a moment like a giant kestrel, before soaring downwind, to land fifty yards away from me.

When in flight like that I would challenge anyone to say they can't understand the sport's appeal. It is a combination of pure majesty and beauty, made all the better because the hawk clearly enjoys it too. For the rest of the session Sioux was a hawk transformed. Like a child or a puppy, I could almost feel his newly-found self-confidence in his powers of flight. He was startlingly obedient in comparison with the last few days when the weather had taken its toll.

The gales that lashed us recently not only severely hampered his exercise, but knocked his *amour-propre* badly. He is still not as fit as he should be and, as a homebred youngster, is a little unsure of himself. His unsteadiness isn't helped by the broad, sail-like wings with which nature has equipped buzzards. In the slightest breeze, these catch the wind, flinging him across the fields. Then he crash lands in bushes and trees, or ends up perched awkwardly on a branch far too small for his weight, flailing around in a mass of twigs.

More alarmingly, sometimes he is scooped up by stronger

gusts and flung over hedgerows and buildings, whisked all-too-quickly out of sight. There is no danger of losing him when this happens – he is still far too unfit for that – but having to run after your bird is not exactly what falconry is supposed to be about. Besides, the experience inevitably leaves him rattled and in a bad mood: certainly unwilling to risk a long flight or chance his wings in a stiffish breeze.

Nevertheless, we continue to make progress and it has lifted my spirits. They have been boosted further by the awareness that he has been cheered up too. A growing confidence in his own powers of flight has produced an almost magical transformation in his attitude to our sessions together. Apparently he now realises that we are a team and that he can look forward to our time together.

Thursday 28 January

I WENT YESTERDAY to visit a local falconer called Jack who I'd heard about by word of mouth from a friend of a friend of someone who sometimes comes into the pub. That's the way that things happen around here. You want someone to do something? Ask at the pub and they'll give you the name and address. I mentioned the hawk to someone before Christmas and Jack's was the name that came up. At the time I was full of beer and the season, so I merely scribbled the number on a scrap of paper which was thrust into my wallet. A couple of days ago I found it and, by now keen for any help I can get, phoned him.

He was at first slightly suspicious. I can't blame him. The world of falconry has a fair number of undesirables, light-fingered opportunists ready to take advantage of lax security or flimsy pens to steal birds worth hundreds of pounds. But as we talked, he gradually realised I was genuine, if ignorant, and seemed to warm to me. He concluded the chat with an invitation to visit him, an offer which I leaped at.

A glance at the dirt and grime of the yard showed it was clearly a working farm, with ancient tractors rusting under ramshackle lean-tos. Turkeys, chickens and ducks wandered disconsolately across the mud and three damp terriers rushed yapping to the car door as I got out.

Jack was nothing like the person I had pictured during the phone conversation. The previous night his voice had seemed very old and upper-class. I pictured him as a tweed-clad gentleman, one who had taken up falconry in old age as an interesting pastime to entertain the 'fellas in the club'. I had felt sure he was someone who had retired after a successful career in one of the professions.

Instead I was presented with a man who looked considerably younger than I had imagined: probably about fifty I guessed (in reality it turned out to be sixty). Wild grey hair lay tangled over his head. Some strands brushed his shoulders and a pair of wire-framed spectacles perched on his forehead, forming a crude hairgrip. He was wearing an ancient Arran sweater which might once have been white, but was now grey and brown with grime. Ragged holes were worn in its elbows, snags of wool hung from the front. A tatty pair of ancient cords graced his legs, again decorated with toil-generated holes. Through these I could see his legs.

His face was red from a lifetime in the country and three of his teeth were missing. He held a massive wooden plane in his hands, one of the old-fashioned sort, curls of clean, new timber spilling from its well. Fresh sawdust clung all over him. In spite of the cold he was panting and looked hot.

It turns out that he is a genuine farmer and part-time carriage restorer (horse-drawn that is) in addition to being a passionate falconer. Naturally, in spite of the beautiful cart he proudly showed me within the first minute of my arrival, I had eyes and ears only for his birds. He has six of these: three sakers, a pair of peregrines and a tiercel goshawk. Although Sioux is far from ugly, Jack's birds are spectacular, in particular his falcon.

I use the term advisedly. The pedantic textbooks point out that a falcon is really a female peregrine and that to use it for any other species of longwinged raptor is incorrect, let alone to describe a male. She is a cross between a barbary falcon and a peregrine (the former is a subspecies of the latter),

57

her flanks and cheeks tinged with a beautiful rosy tint. She and her mate are very small for peregrines – the tiercel flying at little more than a pound (pure-bred females can weigh more than double that). As we peered through a hole in the fence surrounding their breeding quarters, he took to the wing and described an incredibly tight turning circle around the pen. Even in the narrow confines of the enclosure, it was an impressive display of speed and manoeuvrability, the bird flashing around the walls, his rapidly beating wings not even brushing the numerous perches.

As we talked and he sensed my obvious envy, Jack soon proved positively friendly. I had a good two-hour chat with him, besides looking at his breeding quarters, and am to return in a couple of months to have a look at the eyasses. One of his most impressive qualities is a distaste for money when linked to the sport. He scoffs at the thought of selling birds and his love for them goes so far as to have deliberately released goshawks into the Oxfordshire countryside in the past – no mean gesture when one considers that even at today's depressed prices, these can easily fetch £1000. He was motivated by a desire to see them re-established in the area, righting a wrong two centuries old.

But his distaste for filthy lucre goes further.

'I don't approve of people who buy or sell birds,' he said. 'All right, I know you've got to, but however much you pay for your bird, forget about how much it cost. It's a trap that's bad for you, your falcon and your sport. If you think that your bird is worth, say £500, then every time you fly it, you'll see a £500 cheque winging its way away from you.

'The sort of people who fly "expensive" birds are so terrified of flying their hawks that they keep them too low in order to be sure they'll come back,' he continued. 'As a result the bird lacks energy and they never see the thing fly at its best. The bird is too hungry to enjoy flying and the falconer too worried that the thing will bugger off to enjoy the flight properly. It's a mug's game – don't fall into the trap!' He was emphatic, speaking with an earnestness and venom that showed his feeling.

'There are some people who can easily afford the loss of a few hundred quid, but they waste time and effort on a pastime where they count it a success when they've got the bird back in their hand after a day's sport,' he continued. 'It does them and the bird no good at all. I've lost lots of birds, sakers, peregrines and gosses and you take it as part of the game. As long as you know they can look after themselves, there's no problem, you shrug your shoulders and wish them good luck.'

I realised quickly that Jack is very different from the falconers who wrote the books I am using. He is a purist, someone who sticks rigidly to the sport's traditions. He insists on using old-fashioned jesses and a screen perch – both branded as dangerous in modern manuals.

In former years jesses were of only one type – a long strip of supple leather threaded through itself around the hawk's

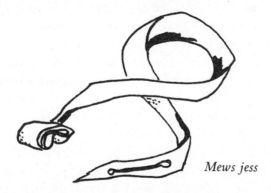

Mews jess

leg. At the end furthest from the bird is a slit to which the swivel is attached. A four-foot leash goes through this and in turn is attached to the perch or glove, preventing the bird from disappearing. When it is time to fly the hawk free, the leash and swivel are removed, leaving just the jesses, which are used to restrain the bird when on the fist.

The basic design dates back to the very origins of the sport, but the problem with these jesses is that it is perfectly possible for the slits to get caught up on a twig, snagging the hawk in a way that is at best disruptive to flying and at worst fatal. If it occurs high up an unclimbable tree, the unfortunate

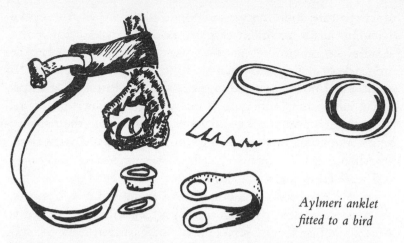

Aylmeri anklet fitted to a bird

bird can hang upside-down to die a lingering death. This was the fate that had almost certainly met White's goshawk and – I hang my head in shame – the kestrel I had nursed back to health so long ago (although in both cases their fates were sealed by escaping complete with jesses, swivel and leash).

Early this century, however, an Indian army officer, Guy Aylmer, invented a way of riveting a bracelet around the hawk's leg, allowing interchangeable buttoned leather strips to be used. The advantage of this system is that, should the bird escape or get lost, sooner or later the jesses will be pulled out, leaving the hawk unencumbered. Better still, one can change the slitted 'mews' jesses for the similar, but slitless, 'field' variety. These are almost impossible to snag and thus safer for the bird, while still allowing the falconer to hang on to the bird until he wants it to leave the fist. No one wants to lose a hawk, but it's unforgivable to see it condemned to death as it rediscovers its liberty.

But Jack refuses such new-fangled additions to the sport: 'Don't like 'em, won't use 'em,' he barked when I noted the jesses on his moulting saker, hooded and tethered on its own. 'By the time you've put anklets and rivets and bells and bewits and jesses on the hawk, it's a wonder the bloody thing can get off the ground. I only put one bell on my birds and use jesses that are so thin it's a miracle they don't snap.'

As we talked I felt almost shocked to learn that he goes

much further in his insistence on tradition. I had read that 'hacking' has long since been abandoned, but apparently not. This is the practice of giving eyasses complete freedom for their first few days or weeks of flight. The youngsters are fed regularly at one site and their progress is monitored carefully to see which is fastest, which most confident and, most vital of all, which is first to make a kill. When this last happens – or when the falconer fears the youngsters are becoming too proficient or self-confident to fly free any longer – they are recaptured and training begins.

In the past, when hawks were vermin and it was easy to obtain a whole nest of eyasses, hacking was standard practice, the inevitable losses covered by releasing three or four together. My books said it is unheard of nowadays: birds are too valuable to be risked in this way and even if they were, the experts query its advantages. Certainly the birds may become confident and learn how to kill, but they can also learn bad habits too, such as becoming 'wedded' to the wrong quarry.

But Jack still hacks.

'Makes a much better hawk,' he said. 'But I do it mainly because I love to see them flying around the farm.'

I made the mistake of saying that I had thought this was now frowned on by the experts.

'Which "experts" are you talking about? Not that lot in Gloucestershire or Kent?' he snapped, referring to the two authors I was thinking of. 'They're not falconers – they may know a lot about breeding birds in zoo conditions, but they know bugger all about falconry. You've got to hunt with your hawks, fly them at quarry, not dried wings on a bit of string.'

I felt a bit cowed. He was clearly irritated by the mere thought of the scattering of falconry centres around the country. 'They don't hack their birds because they're scared of losing them. They think of birds as money, no true falconer does that.'

Mind you, even a purist makes some concessions to the modern age: however much Jack may love seeing hawks flying free around his farm, not even he can afford to lose too many birds. He uses telemetry on his falcons and goshawks, fitting a tiny transmitter to their tails so that in the event of a disaster he can track their progress and, with luck, recover them.

'You wouldn't need it on your red tail,' he said. 'They're such slow, lazy creatures, but you need it on a saker. They can travel five miles in as many minutes if they take off after a pigeon. They're fast enough to catch them as well – and that's bloody fast!' He cackled at the thought. 'My falcon caught one a couple of weeks back. By the time I found her she'd had it all. Without the transmitter I'd never have got her back.' His good humour was by now thoroughly recovered and he was rattling away, a gap-toothed grin splitting his face. I muttered quietly that I certainly had no need of a tracking device: the racket that Sioux makes is more reliable than any telemetry.

'He's an imprint is he?' asked Jack. I nodded glumly.

'Well then, it's particularly important to enter him fast,' he advised. 'Sometimes – but only sometimes – they shut up when they get killing: they're murderous bastards and it cheers 'em up no end.'

As we spoke I found myself curiously depressed. He has already put all his birds into their mews for the moult and the thought that this will soon affect Sioux is disturbing. Although it still seems very early in the year, the mating season is well under way. Pheasants are the loudest, crowing their defiance across the valley. One particularly spectacular cock lives in the field above the cottage and over the past few days I have been watching him out of the window every day, his bright orange and gold plumage still gleaming in spite of his own approaching moult. His head is a splendid deep dark green, burnished with a metallic sheen.

I have always loved cottage springs, relishing those long afternoons lying in the lush grass, buried below its surface, disappearing beneath the shimmering waves rippled across its surface by the wind. But this year the appeal is even greater, the dread of leaving worse: and leave I must at Easter when my parents will want their cottage back. Although Sioux has to moult, this won't take all summer and the thought of being forced to watch him sitting in his pen in Islington but unable to fly is truly dreadful.

All this flashed through my mind as I talked to Jack, surrounded by the ramshackle buildings of a working farm. Peacocks, turkeys, chickens and ducks pecked around our feet as we talked, a couple of pointers and the terriers wandered across the bare earth of the yard while a bitter north wind flicked pieces of broken straw over the hard-packed earth. It was freezing and I could feel my teeth beginning to chatter as the conversation rambled on. I didn't dare mention my discomfort, however, lest it end a conversation I should have had months ago. Here at last was the chance to ask all those questions that the books forgot to answer, to fill in some of the many gaps.

The Americans insist on beginners being apprenticed for two years to an experienced falconer and as I talked to Jack I could see the value of the rule. I got more out of an hour's chat with him than out of countless hours spent scouring my battered falconry manuals. A two-year apprenticeship seems a touch on the tough side, but it has definite advantages over the situation here. When the powers-that-be rightly decided the law concerning captive birds needed tightening up, there were two clear alternatives: either regulate the birds or owners. After hours of careful scrutiny they chose, wrongly. The Wildlife and Countryside Act (1981) says that anyone not convicted of an offence of animal cruelty can own a bird of prey, provided that it is properly documented – which in practice means bred in captivity. This means that any idiot can – and all too frequently does – buy something about which he or she knows little or nothing. Sadly the cheapest species are also some of the most difficult – usually because they are the smallest and least useful for falconry. The most notable example is the sparrowhawk, where the musket (male), at half the size of the female, is frequently given away by breeders only too glad to be rid of him. He is so tiny and highly strung that even the most experienced falconers fight shy of attempting to fly him. Weighing as little as four ounces, the slightest error results in death for the tiny bird – a shade too thin and he's dead from starvation, too heavy by the same margin and he's lost, probably to die from hunger unless he's already an accomplished killer (unlikely in the hands of a beginner).

And the Government did the same thing a few years later when it came to legislating on dangerous dogs. In both cases it was simplest to regulate the animal rather than the human, but the old cliché comes to mind: 'there are no bad animals, only bad owners'. I don't think that I've been a bad beginner, but talking to Jack I couldn't help thinking that forcing me to take advice would have been a good idea.

Friday 29 January

ONE IMPORTANT RESULT of the visit to Jack is that I have finally had a long conversation I've been meaning to have for weeks. I phoned up the local pest control officer. Chris used to be gamekeeper to the trust which runs the estate, but since it ceased to let out the shooting as a commercial concern, his attentions have been turned to keeping the rabbits, squirrels and crows under control. Mind you, this still doesn't stop him from trying to nourish the available game on the estate.

I enquired about getting permission to fly the hawk on his patch, extending my hunting territory dramatically from the scraps of land around the cottage. Most of the knowledgeable locals seemed to think that permission to fly the hawk at rabbits would be almost automatic and Jack in particular was certain it would be granted. Indeed, he was insistent that one should ask before even thinking about it. With so much encouragement, I phoned Chris and introduced myself by way of the various local people who had suggested I talk to him. He said, in his turn, that he'd heard of me too. Not surprising, I suppose, in such a small community. In theory he said I could fly on his patch and pointed me towards a couple of good local sites.

Oddly enough, the place that he thinks most likely to produce results is one which I discovered only last week. After the car failed to start due to a flat battery I had to walk into town. With the dogs in tow I was reluctant to walk along the road and a glance at a map showed a path, the existence of which I'd been oblivious to until that point. As I walked along the track a glance to the side showed a hedgerow a couple of hundred yards away, the base of which seemed suspiciously bare of grass: a tell-tale sign that something – probably rabbits – was present in large numbers. Sure enough, as I watched, first one and then a second lolloped into view. The sighting lifted my hopes, although at that point I had no idea who owned the land.

Chris was interested in the hawk, but he was still concerned for his pheasants. It is important that they're not frightened with the breeding season approaching and he doesn't want them terrified and put off laying. I was at pains to stress (with reasonable truth) that the hawk wouldn't bother them as Jack had warned me to do. This seemed to reassure him, but he then told me that I would have to wait until permission was formally granted by the lawyers responsible for running the estate trust. Until that was forthcoming, he suggested that I talk to the other part of the estate, which, for complex tax reasons, is run in a completely different way.

We progressed to a conversation in general terms about the local wildlife. The reports I've been hearing about buzzards breeding locally are true, it turns out. At one point last summer it seems that seven could be seen circling together on the other side of the estate. He was happy enough about these and the other raptors on his beat, although, when pressed, he admitted that the number of sparrowhawks was a slight worry: 'It's nice to see a few about,' he said. 'But they do take a toll of the local birds and they are, to be honest, a bit of a headache.'

That was last night and the thought led to me staying awake for longer than usual as I lay in bed, dreaming of hunting them with Sioux. As often happens on these occasions, good news comes in clusters. I had an even more promising opening this morning through a chance meeting with my next door neighbour. Anne and her husband are farmers and, it turns out, own a well-populated warren that I discovered last summer.

One hot July evening, Dill and I had left her puppies to go for a walk. I had no idea where we would go, but our ramble became more focused as we strolled along. It was as if the heat drew us like a magnet to the river. And on the way, near an old mill, we stumbled on a tiny, long-abandoned quarry whose steep sides have left it an oasis of untouched land in a desert of cultivation.

There are huge holes at one end which I suspect are the work of badgers, but that evening there was no sign of them. Instead the place was alive with rabbits, and many of the younger ones, never having seen humans, allowed us to approach quite close before flitting into the myriad of holes. I wasn't counting, but guess we saw fifty or so in the space of ten minutes. Given that many more must be underground, I reckoned that this must mean a warren of at least two hundred.

All those rabbits proved far more important than I could have suspected. It was the sight of these that was one of the indirect reasons that led to Sioux's acquisition by prompting one of my biannual 'hawk crises'. I reached for my well-thumbed falconry books, as I have done so regularly over the years. I pored over the text, dreaming of ownership, my hypnotic fascination for raptors re-awoken by the flashing white scuts.

Originally I thought of a sparrowhawk, the plan being to release it at the end of the summer, hacking it back into the wild to join its wild brothers and sisters. There were various arguments against this, however. To begin with, even I thought I might have trouble with one of these tiny and highly-strung killers and the sight of those white tails clinched it. These are beyond the capabilities of all but the largest and most determined of female spars, and I dreamed of getting permission to hunt these rabbits, of returning home exhausted after a morning crunching through the frost. In my dreams, a vital player was a big, well-trained hawk, hurtling after them.

Today, as I remember how recently I was even considering it, I shudder at the near miss. If I have been having all these problems with a buzzard (and am still to enter him), what sort of a mess would I have made of the smaller bird?

Fortunately, I avoided the mistake, passing the pitfall in blissful ignorance and only now have I realised the danger. But the general idea stayed to germinate, the hawk was acquired, and now here I was with the hawk on my fist, walking back from a training flight towards the cottage as Anne returned home. She was just in time to see him plummet on to my fist and she pulled up her car to chat. As so often, Sioux's magic worked: she volunteered to ask her husband if he would let me fly the hawk at the rabbits in the quarry. I am finding it hard to contain my excitement. Now he is fit and I have land to hunt on. The last stage of Sioux's training looks set to begin.

Saturday 30 January

I WAS WOKEN this morning by a phone call. Or rather, I was jerked into full consciousness by the phone while lying in bed, dozing and half listening to the radio. It was Chris, the pest control officer again. He had been talking to the estate's agent and said that, if I wrote to him, he was sure permission would be granted. I reassured him further about the hawk and pheasants. Sioux would be moulting during the breeding season, I pointed out, and thus unable to fly. He could not even frighten them, let alone kill any. This cheered him up. Clearly he had been thinking about rabbits too, and he said that he had another couple of spots in mind. 'I want you to have a few places,' he said. 'Just one gets very boring and you might as well get some good sport.' He also warned me against flying the hawk too near the Cheeseford Estate, a vast tract of land mainly comprising the last scrappy remnants of the forest that once cloaked most of southern England.

Cheeseford has a reputation for being unwelcoming

towards uninvited guests, to put it mildly. It is one of the last heavily-keepered local estates. As a child I used to walk there and even discovered a gibbet near one track – the dried, mould-covered corpses of stoats, squirrels and jays serving as a grim reminder of the barbarism of nineteenth-century gamekeeping. Then I heard of a trespasser having his dog shot while it was on a lead and stopped my clandestine visits. Chris and I agreed, tacitly, that the Cheeseford gamekeepers were not a friendly bunch: on his part the point was made mainly with pregnant pauses.

Following the chat, I phoned the keeper on the other half of Chris's estate. He was very friendly, having already been tipped off by his partner, and instantly said I could fly over some of the fields immediately surrounding the village. When permission to fly on the other half of the estate comes through and, touch wood, that of my farmer neighbour, Anne, I will be able to fly on an area of several square miles – more than I'd ever imagined.

Fuelled by all this good news, I have just driven to look at the wood above the village. I was trying to see if there were any rabbits about, but apart from a big cock pheasant there was nothing visible, not even with my new binoculars. As I turned, I was surprised to see a big dog fox running towards me along the middle of the road. He seemed not at all perturbed to see me in the car, but instead continued coming straight at me. In size I would guess he was only slightly smaller than a lightly-built labrador, perhaps lower at the shoulder, but a bit stockier. He was so intent on his direction as he lolloped quickly along, I thought for a while he might be being pursued by the hounds, but, as I continued, was pleased to see there was no sign of any hunt.

Sunday 31 January

AN OTHERWISE LONELY weekend was interrupted by Dickie who came out today, complete with crashing hangover, on his motorbike. He had left his tools over here a fortnight ago when he came to check over my car for me. I was quite surprised by the level of his interest – after all, I thought, most of his pastimes are mechanical and modern: cars, bikes, computers, windsurfing and mountain biking. But the link turned out to be his obsession with flying. As an amateur pilot he has a natural respect for Sioux's abilities. Although by my recent flights, the hawk was playing up, Dickie was impressed, largely because last time he came out Sioux was barely trained, and the comparison was startling.

Unfortunately, as we strode across a field, the bird took off, heading for the trees above a fox den near some horses. This was a pity. Not only is he still a little slow (trained, but not obedient) and the presence of two of us put him off, but he clearly hates horses. They, in turn, were excited by my whistling and galloped around the field, tossing their manes and stamping their hooves on the frost-hardened soil. It was clear from Sioux's stance that he wanted to come down, but was distracted by the continual whinnying and clatter behind him.

I gave Dickie the glove, gratified by his interest and anxious to encourage his enthusiasm. Sioux showed little interest, however, and after five minutes I held up an arm clothed in my leather jacket in desperation and it was on this that he landed softly. Under the circumstances, I was doubly glad that his 'sticky-footedness' seems to be curing itself as his confidence increases: I had little faith in the jacket's ability to withstand his needle sharp claws and paralysing grip.

He is now showing much less interest in staying up trees and is beginning to 'ladder' up branches, overcoming his dislike of flying when twigs obscure the view. I can feel his confidence rising as his muscles and stamina improve. It seems almost incredible that it is just a week since he began to fly well. Overall today's session was marked by long flights and, even though his returns were a little slow, his behaviour was reasonable. One interesting addition to the day's flight was a long shallow stoop of over a hundred yards or so. But instead of landing, he merely clipped the back of my outstretched fist and flew on and around, describing a wide circle before pitching into the same tree.

There was no improvement in his screaming, however. It has now become a perpetual screeching whenever I am in sight. Given that he can see me for almost all of his flying sessions, this means most of the time. It has a terrible penetrating quality which I am becoming gradually inured to, at least for part of the time. But friends such as Dickie, viewing his training flights, find it almost unbearable: particularly when, as in this case, there are hangovers around.

I keep thinking there are cheering signs on this front too: but am I deluding myself? Occasionally the racket will be punctuated by glorious bouts of silence as he shuts up, with his eyes on the constant *qui vive*, his shoulders slightly hunched as he stares around. I know I am probably grasping at straws, but I can't help hoping against hope that one day he will shut up for ever. I must find some rabbits now as quickly as possible. Jack thinks he might shut up once he gets hunting – although he also made it clear that he thought this unlikely.

I went to bed later than intended. I had prepared a pot of stock from a chicken carcass and put it on to reduce while I went over the Sunday papers. Naturally I forgot about the boiling bones and was lifted abruptly from the intensity of my reading by the appalling smell of burning. The kitchen was full of smoke – the dense, acrid kind, which sweeps into the mouth and catches at the back of the throat. Why is it that destructive smoke is so unpleasant? The smell of a wood fire, bacon or a kipper is pleasant. Even a pipe can produce a dense, heady aroma. But burning flesh is invariably horrible. I opened the doors and windows to release the swirling cloud while 'Sailing By' rang out from the radio.

As I stood in the cottage doorway, all too literally tasting the disaster, I could see him there, hunched in the shed, barely distinguishable in the dark, his white chest just visible through the glass. With his head tucked in under his wing he looked like nothing so much as a headless phantom, decapitated in the gloom.

I could hear the distant sound of running water, while the leaves and branches of the surrounding foliage dripped with moisture. It wasn't raining, but a damp chill hung over the cottage, a sort of rainforest dankness, one in which you might never need to drink, but rather slake your thirst merely by breathing.

It reminded me of a recent source of wonder, the abundance of local springs at the moment, of water spontaneously oozing from the soil and mud of the fields to form little rivers. The rushing that I could hear comes from a hundred yards away, where pure water seeps from the land behind the hut at the bottom of the field, forming a swampy morass. It is here that woodpigeons congregate and the local cock pheasant parades every morning, apparently revelling in the fertility of it all.

It is also the place to which Sioux always seems drawn by the wind whenever I fly him in that part of the field. He heads for the willow branches as if drawn by some powerful magnet and is always slow to come down. In practice I know this is because he dislikes returning if he doesn't have a clear view, but it doesn't feel like that when I am waiting below, slapping the meat against the glove and, all too literally whistling at the wind. As I walk slowly away from him in the hope he will come like a child fearful of being abandoned, it seems as if he is held by the water, drawn to its life-giving qualities.

Monday 1 February

TODAY BEGAN WITH another chance meeting with my neighbour, Anne. She has asked her husband and they've agreed it would be fine for me to hunt in their little quarry. Afterwards I found it difficult to contain my excitement, my thoughts returning time and again to visions that had first appeared last summer.

Eventually, as a magnificent bloody sunset faded behind the woods hemming the horizon, I could at last change Sioux's jesses ready for the trip. This time, as I approached him, he was keen, the first time that I've seen him so fired up. He was bating *towards* me, wings flapping as he tried to take off for the glove. Something has clicked in his malevolent brain

Sioux in
yarak

and he now not only associates my glove with food, but seems positively to look forward to flying and the exercise.

My heart soared. There is a falconry term, 'yarak', which describes a hawk in the perfect frame of mind for hunting. It is most often used of the goshawk, but all raptors have an equivalent state. Might this enthusiasm be Sioux in yarak?

I checked my soaring spirits. It was undoubtedly premature, but I am beginning to sense he is on the point of transforming himself into a proper hunting hawk. Good God, falconry is mesmeric! I am spending more and more of my time thinking, walking and breathing the sport.

Having changed his jesses, I tossed a chick leg into his carrying box and he leaped in after it. With him packaged up and screaming loudly, I drove out to the small lane which leads towards the little quarry.

I parked in a muddy lay-by and got out. He hopped on to my fist readily and we walked down the lane, squelching

72

through the mud that is everywhere at the moment. Unfortunately the field turned out to be ploughed. I trudged across it, my feet getting heavier with every step as the thick Cotswold mud coagulated on the tread of my boots.

With the bloody hawk screaming all the way, there was, I suppose, little hope of catching any rabbits by surprise and sure enough there were none to be seen. In any event someone seems to have been at work, either gassing or ferreting the warren.

But the expedition was not a failure. To begin with he is getting the idea of coming for a walk, happily flying along hedges, and keeping up a fair pace, although mind you, screaming all the while. He is also coming quickly now, flying to the fist with little need for exhortation. At any rate, in contrast with even yesterday, he didn't 'stick' anywhere and we made good progress, as I strode along at my normal pace, the only delays my backward glances to check on his progress. This was normally enough to get him to fly to me.

In general, once we get going, his screaming now seems to die down, particularly towards the end of a session. I am also encouraged by the way he is learning to hop around bushes of his own volition, manoeuvring until he can see a clear enough path to fly to me. Such is my hypnotic fascination with him that every tiny detail gives me an inordinate amount of pleasure.

It was at the very end of the walk, as I contemplated this source of satisfaction, that a further surge of optimism was prompted – not that had anyone else been there they would have noticed this cause for delight. I was trudging across the two small fields, taking a short cut back to the car in the failing light, when I put up a rabbit. It streaked away underneath him – but unfortunately I couldn't see Sioux and his reaction to it. I rushed to the hedge, desperate to see his receding tail as he streaked along the hedge after the disappearing scut. Perhaps he'd catch it?

It is a mark of my obsession that when I saw nothing along the willow-bottoms and, raising my eyes, caught sight of him above me, I was overjoyed. Instead of feeling my optimism and adrenalin dashed, I was encouraged to see him staring intently after it. He was interested; all he lacked was confidence.

So while an expert would no doubt have been unimpressed, I made my way back home feeling pleased with his performance, only to bump into a neighbour in the village. I'd been introduced to Caroline last week by a friend in the newsagent's. She had collected the village children from school and was unloading the clutch. I stopped and showed them the hawk, going so far as to take him out of the box and flying him up to the bush outside the house. This was duly met by gasps from the children and Caroline, but any good impression I might have had of her was significantly marred by her comment: 'Would he like a grape?'

How could a well-educated country-dweller think that a bird of prey would enjoy tucking into fruit? It's on a par with the comments that Jack says are regularly fired at him: 'Does he talk?' being a particular favourite. A glance at his talons (sorry, hawks have claws, falcons talons) and beak would have been sufficient to show his diet was flesh and bone.

But I didn't need to reply as he was already swooping on my glove. 'What's that?' she asked.

'A day-old chick,' I said, matter-of-factly.

The kids duly made puking sounds and their mother blanched. Further questioning on her part established that I was trying to catch rabbits. Again she didn't seem to approve. I tried to excuse myself with the comment that I would gladly eat anything that he killed. I just hope I kept the depths of longing for that meal out of my voice.

I returned to the cottage as dusk was beginning to fall. The dogs were, of course, delighted to see me. It was a pity that I couldn't take them out too, but to have three animals to train simultaneously would be too much. Instead I let them out and, fuelled by some strange energy that came from God knows where, I attacked the compost heap and bonfire. The former I turned over with the fork and was gratified to see it turning into decent mulch, almost, but not quite ready for spreading on the flower beds. I am slightly puzzled, however, by the presence of two or three holes near the top of the pile. They look like tunnels, but God knows what could have made them – they are far too large for a mouse. Perhaps they are caused by the heap gently rotting down, collapsing slowly in on itself, undermined by the billions of bacteria that inhabit it. It is strange to think how such tiny creatures can make such a big physical impact.

I also dug out the bonfire, a much less pleasant chore, the base being comprised of a soggy mixture of leaves, paper, plastic and non-burnable detritus. I had to resort to using my hands, peering through the gloom at the mess as I turned it out, an unpleasant task with scraps of rotting material, which some creature – either a fox or more probably one of the dogs – had scattered around the lawn. I vowed to be more selective, making sure that in future all vegetable and food scraps would go on the compost heap.

With the light almost gone, I looked with affection at the two dogs. The poor saps get exercise out here, but few walks. So I strode off down the valley, the gloom now rapidly darkening. We didn't get too far, of course, it being barely light enough to see what was going on, but the two were happy enough as they scampered along, bouncing over each other, Dill rolling Havoc in the damp grass with shoulder charges.

Their high spirits no longer give me the same pleasure that they used to. Although I have stockbroken Dill, I have never bothered to discourage her from chasing pheasants. She can't catch them; besides, in contrast to worrying sheep or cows, it isn't a crime to allow a dog to scare wild game. Now her instincts are a positive danger, however. By urban standards my dogs are well-trained and under control, but by any rural yardstick they are appallingly behaved. People really object to dogs running free, particularly in the proximity of stock, and the fact that Dill tends to yap excitedly when chasing something doesn't help. Any farmer with sheep for miles around who hears the cacophony must imagine a demented pack of hell-hounds ripping through his flocks.

What has really changed, however, is that I am now dependent on the goodwill of neighbours for my hunting. While in the past I could risk their occasional disapprobation, now I dread losing some of my vital hunting grounds. Slowly the hawk appears to be taking over every aspect of my life, colouring even my attitudes to my two long-standing canine companions.

Tuesday 2 February

I WAS WOKEN by Havoc beginning a rhythmic, hiccuping cough. Anyone who has ever had a dog will know the sound. A glance at the rippling muscular contractions spreading in waves down her neck revealed it as one of the most powerful stimulants there is. Forget ear-piercing alarms, double espressos or even the door being kicked down by armed police – the knowledge that the dog curled up next to your head is about to vomit wakes you up quicker than anything I know. I was halfway down the stairs in an instant, my long-john clad legs whirling like something out of a cartoon, barely touching the steps as I hurled my body down the house, yelling to both dogs to follow as I went.

It was only partially successful. She managed to get to the first floor landing before coughing up a (mercifully small) little pile. It was 8.45 – far later than I'd intended to get up of course, but still only an hour or so after the sun had risen. I made a cup of tea and overcoming my strong urge to return to bed, remained upright. By nine I was ready to take the hawk out for a flight. The first was at the lure – something that still barely raises his interest. He hesitated for far too long before landing on it. Even a suicidal rabbit, weighed down by the cares of family and world and desirous of ending it all, would have changed its mind by the time he took the plunge. Undaunted by this setback I set off across the paddock above the cottage, walking along the hedgerow up to the road, crossing it and wandering up to the corner of the spinney behind the village. He flew along with me obediently. I deliberately only gave him the heads and legs of the four chicks,

76

however, keeping back what I estimate to be about a half ration for another session this afternoon at dusk.

Needless to say, neither bout produced any fruit. In part this was due to the weather, which was damp if not actually raining, and must be the result of the continual racket that advertises our presence. The main problem, however, seems to be a combination of too few rabbits and the terrain, which has too much cover. With most of the surrounding fields ploughed, there is nothing to tempt the creatures out into the open and in consequence they are rarely more than two yards from dense undergrowth. I saw a couple of scuts disappearing, a few shadows flitting through the trees and heard some scuffles, but Sioux seemed oblivious to all of this. The books blithely tell me to engineer a good chance for a first kill by finding a rabbit a long way from cover, preferably a young one. If only! . . .

Wednesday 3 February

THIS MORNING, HE continued to perform well, flying greater and greater distances with shorter and shorter hesitations. He is getting used to the idea of 'hedge-hopping' without coming to the fist, although he still has a tendency to fly close to me *en route*. Once or twice this forced me into an undignified duck as it became clear that he was about to land on my head when the fist was not forthcoming.

Since then I have spent a disconsolate day attempting to begin a novel. With an alarming absence of work, I need to do something between my two daily hawk flights. As a result I began research on a thriller to be set locally. The idea is to set it in one of the villages abandoned after the Black Death and I was attempting some preliminary research on place names. The results were surprising. Although I had always known that Oxfordshire has been occupied by man for many centuries, I was still taken aback to find that every local place name appears in the Doomsday Book.

But more interesting is a history of the local parish that I found covered in dust on one of the shelves. A little prim and proper, it is nevertheless well-written and researched. Among the snippets of information I discovered was that in 1278, among the parish's fifty-five householders was a village falconer. It is oddly pleasing to think that seven hundred years ago a predecessor was trudging these same fields, scouring hedgerows for quarry and, who knows, cursing his bird as I curse Sioux.

In a similarly predatory vein, also present among the six free tenants was the forester, Thomas le Venur, while in 1435 William Weller, the warrener, was paid to make a burrow in Le Ferne (probably a local field) to encourage rabbits to nest. This was an interesting reminder that rabbits were not only a valued – and expensive – source of meat during the Middle Ages, but that they were also finding difficulties establishing themselves in the countryside. Professional warreners were needed to protect them from predators and even, as in this case, to build burrows for them.

Relatively soon after this they were becoming well-established because the tell-tale 'Conygree' (Middle English for a place where rabbits were farmed) appears on some maps of the area. Another name which reveals their presence and exploitation is the scrap of woodland which is still called The Warren (although this is, I suspect from its beeches, a late-eighteenth or early nineteeth-century creation by some landlord). The name means that this was originally a place where rabbits were kept in semi-domestication, enclosed and farmed for their meat, skins and fur. I doubt whether they ever reached the numbers around here that they achieved in the great East Anglian warrens like Lakenheath where 128,856 rabbits were killed in 1920/21 and 123,928 the following year.

In many ways this was of course a very sensible use of the land. As their abundance on many Scottish islands bears testimony, they thrive on marginal land where even the toughest breeds of sheep find the going hard. They are good converters of grass into meat – better than sheep or cows – and their flesh is now reckoned to be extremely healthy, low in cholesterol and fat. Naturally they are also entirely free range and thus would appear an excellent foodstuff for today's health-conscious Britain.

Even so, it is unlikely that we will ever see such forms of farming again. To begin with the law now sees the rabbit almost entirely as a pest. After two centuries of agricultural improvements which were boosted by the 'Dig For Victory' campaign, land which once was marginal is now highly productive. In general the food value of a few rabbits on farmland is outweighed by the destruction that they cause.

The industrial revolution was another important factor. It shifted the balance of power from the countryside to the towns. Wealth increasingly owed its roots to trade and manufacturing rather than the land and the idea of the 'natural leader' as a country squire, a man of leisure who spent his days hunting, shooting and fishing, was largely a thing of the past.

Naturally field sports continued to enjoy popularity – this was after all the heyday of the gamekeeper and the big estates – but their nature had changed. No longer content to rough shoot, the gentleman now shot driven birds at weekends – killing them with the same precision and in the same numbers as his factories turned out goods during the week.

In some ways the rabbit embodied this change in attitudes. While rising wages made small-scale harvesting of rabbits uneconomic, the warrens remained an exception and a major industry was built around these. When thousands of the creatures could be caught by one man in a night, the meat was a cheap alternative to farm animals. The skins could be tanned for leather and the hair used to make the felt for bowler hats. Nothing was wasted: even the guts and trimmings from the tanneries were used as fertiliser. By the 1950s there was an industry around the humble rabbit which, in today's terms, would be worth £2bn.

The Second World War did some damage to rabbit as a food stuff. Along with corned beef and spam, it became linked inextricably with notions of rationing and second-rate foodstuffs. But the final blow came with the arrival of 'myxi' in 1953. Rabbit corpses were scattered across the countryside; while their still living, but blind relatives hopped to pathetic deaths. Add newspaper scares about a housewife in Birmingham catching the disease (medically impossible), and it was the end of rabbit pie as a staple evening meal.

Today their numbers are beginning to approach past heights, but few town dwellers will look at them as a food. Among those too young to associate it with days of rationing or the disease, *Watership Down* and Bugs Bunny have made a sentimental impact. Today even Beatrix Potter's *Tale of Benjamin Bunny* looks brutal and callous. It seems ironic that while anthropomorphic trends have sanitised children's literature of any hint of animal death, by the time they are eighteen they will have seen thousands of violent human deaths acted out on screen.

The result of all this is going to be interesting. As the rabbit population explodes back to pre-myxi levels, for the time being there is little to control them. Weasels, stoats and buzzards, for long the major natural predators, are rarer than they were. Foxes may still be plentiful, but they have learned to take other prey. Until rabbits reach plague numbers, or the public learns to appreciate the meat as a delicacy, man will not feel impelled to control them. Already there are ominous rumblings from some farmers of the need to find a new means of control, perhaps enlisting genetic engineering to help in the search for a check on their numbers. It is not imminent – the Australian Government has been searching for over a century for a way to *exterminate* the rabbit there and has yet to find the answer.

The best that anyone could manage was the discovery of myxi: a disease that is naturally endemic in South America where the local fauna has long since become immune to its effects. After a series of unsuccessful attempts to introduce the disease, in 1950 it was introduced to the Murray Valley in New South Wales and within a couple of years it was estimated that 80 per cent of the country's rabbits had been killed. In 1952 a French doctor imported it to control the damage on his estate outside Paris and it spread like wildfire across the continent. Hopping the Channel was no problem, with Kent farmers only too keen to control the depredations on their crops. By 1953 it was here and within months outbreaks were being reported all across the country. At its most virulent the disease has a mortality rate of 99.5 per cent (compared with the Black Death's 25 to 50 per cent) and as the rabbit disappeared so the countryside changed. Downs, once cropped short were now overgrown, many of the animals dependent on the rabbit for food became scarce, and the same farmers who had shot and snared the creatures with enthusiasm began to bemoan its passing.

The impact of their disappearence was great, but even this is now being undone. As rabbit numbers recover, polecats and stoats are returning to the countryside and foxes are rediscovering rabbits rather than berries, earthworms, voles and domestic stock that have dominated the vulpine diet since the Fifties. There is, indeed, evidence that this may be happening around here. I saw my first stoat in a decade this autumn and until last summer I'd never seen a buzzard locally.

As a non-farmer and falconer, musing on the the rabbit's return has cheered me up no end and gone some way to compensate for a set-back in the bird's training. I seem to have cut his weight down just a bit too far. As I walked back to the house to weigh him this afternoon, carelessly changing his jesses as I walked, he was so screaming keen that he grabbed my right hand which was covered by a fingerless woollen glove. Fortunately he failed to connect with my flesh, but his claws locked in the glove. I managed to extract my hand from the glove through which his foot was clenched tightly and continued to change the jesses, assuming he would relax and release the glove. Instead he bated. Pulling himself free of my clutch, he flew up on to the kitchen roof. He screamed and screamed, the woollen glove still skewered in his clenched foot, oblivious to my entreaties. Indeed, his screeches only got worse as I got nearer.

It became clear that he was mantling over what he regarded as his 'kill', furious with me and fearful I might deprive him of it – a sure sign of an imprint, warn the books. As I watched from a distance he tore furiously at the limp scrap of cloth with claws and beak, jingling as his bells chimed to the stamping of his feet. It took ages, but in the end I managed to lure him down, a process followed by an unseemly struggle to extract the glove from his still bunched foot. Needless to say, the session that followed was somewhat soured by this – not I hasten to add on my part, but on his – and in the end I abandoned the effort.

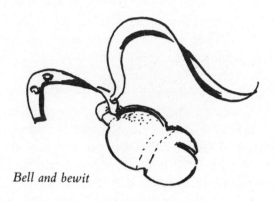

Bell and bewit

Part Two

ENTERING

Thursday 4 February

SIOUX IS NOW a killer. I mean literally a killer as opposed
to a psychotic monster, something he has been ever since he
chipped his way out of the egg. I finally managed to get up
at dawn, reluctantly forcing myself upright into the chilly
bedroom air. By eight I was ready to take him for an early
morning trip. Unfortunately, however, his weight has been
fluctuating more than it ought recently. In my inexperience I
have yet to discover how much food will balance the increased
calorific demands of two daily flights and the effects of the
cold weather. Whatever the answer, if just under two chicks
is sufficient to keep him going indefinitely when tethered to
his perch in the warm, then the equivalent of four is too much
when flying – even in an icy snap.

As a result, this morning he weighed 850g, as opposed to
the 820g which seems to bring out the best in him. Ignoring
this minor hitch, I took him up and was heading for the car
and a trip to the quarry when I spotted a mouse in one of the
catch-'em-alive traps. The temptation was too much. I picked
it up and carried it outside, allowing Sioux to flap off on to
the wall while I headed into the field.

I went a good twenty or thirty yards away from him and
tipped the mouse out. There was of course no hope of him

catching the thing – he was too fat, too far away and had never shown any real interest in chasing anything, not even the temptingly garnished lure.

The mouse was hale and hearty, behaving exactly as one would expect. It streaked away quickly and I could certainly never have recaptured it. Incredibly, however, Sioux, who at that weight would normally be very lethargic, was on it in an instant: and I mean instant. The mouse couldn't have got more than seven or eight yards before the white and brown-streaked feathered bundle of malevolence was on him. There was no mistake, no jiggling and no mantling. Instead, within a couple of seconds the mouse was in his beak, still wriggling with death's nervous twitches. From leaving the trap to hitting his crop couldn't have taken more than five seconds.

Some hawks stop screaming when they start hunting apparently. No such luck with Sioux, who continued to cry out with every bit as much gusto as he gulped it down. As the tail disappeared into his beak, he wobbled his head around with the curious circular motion that he uses to ease food's passage down his throat. Mind you, there was a new element to the way he kept an eye on his surroundings from then on. He stared intently at everything that was going on, particularly the dew-covered grass beneath my wellied feet.

Feeling not a little guilty and sorry for the mouse, I boxed him up and drove to the quarry. But he wasn't flying well, being too slow for my new, higher standards. I gave up after a couple of attempts, returning to the car. The problem is that a mouse is about a half-day's ration and being slightly overweight, the edge had gone from his appetite even if his confidence was greatly boosted.

I am bothered by the death incident. Somehow it doesn't seem quite fair. Mind you, logically it isn't that unfair – I could have been using 'break-back' traps in the kitchen, for example, in which case he'd have been dead from the word go. Also, I deliberately let him go at a distance from the bird that I thought would ensure his escape. I certainly didn't expect Sioux to be quite so efficient. At thirty yards, I thought the rodent would tear off, exciting his interest, but little else, particularly given that he has never killed anything – apart from my glove yesterday, that is.

In addition, if it's any consolation, death when it came was extremely swift and, unlike many trapped mice, at least it served two utilitarian purposes. Not only did it feed the hawk, but it helped to lift his ability to hunt and look after himself should he ever escape.

Nevertheless, I feel pretty shitty about it all. In spite of having the hawk to hunt with, I don't relish the idea of killing things. The purpose of falconry is the challenge of training a wild creature, bending it to my way of thinking and for the thrill of the chase, rather than 'scoring' deaths. It reminds me of a quotation in one of my better-written falconry books:

> One of my peregrines once chased a gull for over 19 minutes by the wrist-watch. Although the distance covered from start to finish was not much over half a mile, the actual mileage flown must have been very considerable indeed. It was an aerobatic display of the highest order, and a fine example of the difference that lies between shooting and falconry, since the fact that the quarry escaped did, if any-thing, enhance the flight.*

Perhaps this explains my sense of unease. So while I am delighted to find that the malevolent lump I have been training for four months really does have a killing instinct and that he is clearly capable of performing well enough, I am not at peace. Somehow it was all over too quickly and the match so uneven that no one could have derived any pleasure from it.

I am also uncomfortably aware that my actions may have been technically illegal – if accidental. The use of 'bagged quarry' (animals released deliberately in front of hunters, be they guns, dogs or hawks) has been outlawed for decades. I have a nasty suspicion that what I did comes into this cate-gory. But breaking the letter of the law is a minor consider-ation – a much bigger source of guilt is the fact that the mouse had never had a chance, let alone a sporting one.

* Phillip Glasier, *Falconry and Hunting*, Batsford, 1978

Still guilt-ridden, I finally got around to watching the video I had bought at the same time as the hawk. It was a disappointment. An American film, it made much of having been passed by a qualified biologist, but whoever vetted this didn't know what they were doing: for example, how can an eyass red tail be 'weaned'?

The makers had also taken too many short-cuts. In contrast to the excellent natural history unit of the BBC, one could feel the financial backers breathing down the necks of the producers. Wild hawks were tempted within camera range by baiting, with the fishing-line holding the carcass down clearly visible in some shots.

Worse, in others, they had live pigeons tethered to attract the more fastidious raptors like goshawks. Although this may be legal in the US, I find it repugnant. The poor bird, fastened to the ground, can do nothing other than flutter about wildly, attracting the attention of marauding raptors and end up very dead. If I had felt bad about the death of a mouse, watching this video was much more distasteful.

And even worse, a pigeon fluttering in a fishing-line harness is a shortcut which will inevitably alter the behaviour of the birds. This undermines any educational value that the film might have. Good nature filming should show genuinely wild predators and prey, with both acting naturally. To bait is to intercede and to distort reality.

But much the most irritating – and the reason I mention all this – was the anthropomorphic narration. A hawk is a bird, not a person, but the words fell into the familiar trap of attributing human emotions to the subjects. It was from the Disney school of natural history films – 'Johnny' the cougar chases deer, yet never succeeds on camera. Somehow, however, he continues to grow, thrive and survive. Heaven help us if the public should see real blood – it might knock the ratings, or worse, upset the advertisers. So instead we see a sanitised version of the wild.

In contrast the work of the BBC natural history unit is something of which we should be justly proud. *The Trials of Life*, for example, was one of the all-time greats. In particular one sequence springs to mind: killer whales hunting sea-lions off the Patagonian coast. In spite of the 'sweetness' of the prey, the film showed the orcas chasing them out of the sea – and then, incredibly, up on to the beach, propelling their thirty-foot, ten-tonne bodies, on to the shore along channels in the shingle, to seize their prey in full, gory Technicolor. Then the unfortunate sea-lion (at eight foot long, no toy), was taken out to sea to be played with, its corpse thrown high into the air and swatted dozens of yards by giant tails, time and time again. It was clear the victim was still alive and making desperate and pathetic attempts to escape the whale's jaws.

The sequence was of course deeply unpleasant. But it was also an awesome display of power and it is the way nature works. To use Blake's words that by now have become a cliché, it is *nature red in tooth and claw*. Sanitising the reality of life, where everything is the potential prey of something else, does no favours to wildlife in the long-run, but leads instead to further manipulation of the environment. If all humankind becomes vegetarian for example, what is to happen to the myriad of farm animals? What of the balance of nature, where herbivore eats grass, defecates, is eaten by carnivore which then dies, is eaten by worms who re-fertilise the soil? Take away any part of the chain and something has to take its place. In this particular case, remove the carnivore and the herbivores multiply, strip the land bare, turning it into desert and *everything* starves to death.

Certainly intensive farming could be more considerate to animals, but some deaths are not only natural, but positively desirable. The problem is that we are distancing ourselves from our food. We are reared on meat that is not only killed by someone else, but, with the rise of the supermarket, increasingly comes packaged in forms that are deliberately disguised. At best this means being displayed wrapped in cling-film on polystyrene trays, but still recognisable as flesh. At worst it is pulped and reconstituted, minced and moulded into the disguised 'chicken nuggets' and 'golden drummers'. If you add the sanitised Disney view of nature to this, is it any wonder that the public becomes confused about death?

Mind you it is unfair to lay the whole blame on modern eating habits. There is more to it than that. One big factor is evident in the local church – an unassuming, quintessentially English, parish church. It is not an outstanding example of its type, but I have always loved the marble carvings on the tombs up by the altar. There are two intricately carved skulls on one, a beautiful standing skeleton on another, and on a third a serpent is swallowing its tail (a traditional symbol of eternity). In all three cases the workmanship is exquisite, particularly the skeleton, which has always been my favourite. I cannot look at them without thinking of the hours of care and attention which must have gone into it. The rib cage is so thin – one slip and the whole piece would have been ruined. Beneath lie the marble effigies of a sixteenth-century local squire and his wife. Alongside are the tiny sculptures of their children, seven or eight in all, carved to represent the ages at which they died. The three smallest are barely a foot long.

The decorations are telling when compared with the modern tombs outside. While the older ones inside say clearly that their occupants are dead, returned to dust and cut down in their prime, all spelt out in intricate beauty, the tombstones outside are made of synthetic, brash black and red reconstituted stone, and seem artificial and crude. On these there are coy phrases like: 'Just sleeping'. They are desperate attempts to avoid the reality of death. Our ancestors, however, were surrounded by it (nine children in the case of one couple). They could not pretend that life is anything other than finite.

As a result, while former villagers had good cause to expect death sooner than their descendants, it held fewer terrors. With their skeletons, skulls and serpents, they marked their passing with clear references to the process of decay. Why the difference? Probably because, as improvements in medicine and diet lengthen life expectancy, the prospect of death recedes. It is now healthy to expect to be alive next year rather than thanking one's lucky stars for surviving the night.

Sunday 7 February

THE OBSESSION WITH THE BIRD has now reached ludicrous proportions. The importance of the weather when exercising him has become crucial and I have begun to find myself trying to plan ahead for the next day by listening to one of the three or four detailed radio forecasts. Glancing at my watch I drop everything at five to eight, one, and six, with the half-past midnight slot most important of all. It worries me. I mean, it is all very well to be enthralled by the hawk, to admire his beauty, to love flying him and look forward to hunting – but there is something disturbing when this extends to weather forecasts. Surely these must be the most boring programmes on the radio? I certainly find it hard to think of a competitor. But here I am, listening enthralled, three or four times a day. Everything else ceases as I sit there, concentrating with rapt attention as a faceless voice intones a monotonal prediction.

I find it amazing that they can get away with it. As a journalist I was always trained to start with a catchy introduction – the one liner, the paradox, the snappy quote. Weather forecasters seem to have been trained in reverse. Instead of grabbing the attention of the audience, they seem determined to lose as many listeners as possible. Hence the crucial information about the next day only comes after a lengthy analysis of the previous day's weather. Two minutes into the broadcast, it lasts five seconds, and then the voice moves on to Scotland and the North.

So, in spite of the importance of the information, I am totally incapable of catching the prediction for tomorrow. However hard I try, as the opening words hit my ears, within seconds, my mind is on the hawk instead. Invariably by the time I've realised what I am doing and snap back to reality, it is only to hear the words 'Northern Ireland and Scotland north of the Great Glen will experience very different conditions . . .'

Monday 8 February

SIOUX IS NOW raring to hunt. He proved it when I took him for a flight with another friend, Martin, who was here on a weekend escape from London. He has just been made redundant and although normally an ebullient character, has been depressed lately. The countryside seemed a natural anti-dote. Although he is a town-dweller, born and bred, he was fascinated by the hawk and thrilled when I asked if he wanted to see a training session.

We walked along the hedgerows towards the remains of what was once a medieval village, but today is merely a rough, unploughed patch of grass and scrub. As the hawk landed in one ivy-covered stump, he suddenly flung himself at something. There was a commotion and a squirrel shot out from under his feet, tearing along the branches and into another tree swathed in ivy. It was only a small one, three-quarters grown and probably not more than a couple of months old.

The incident certainly got to Sioux and he spent the next ten minutes flapping around the tree, peering intently at the foliage, his amber eyes boring through the cover and body tensed for action. He was so wired up as I attempted to dislodge the thing, tapping on the side of the tree with a piece of fallen – and rotten – wood, that when this broke in two he was on it in an instant, pouncing as it bounced across the bare earth. He then proceeded to run around the tree with the peculiar bouncing gait of a creature designed to propel itself with wings rather than legs. In the commotion he stopped shrieking too; raising the tiny remaining hopes I still harbour that he might shut up if he gets hunting successfully.

If Sioux was excited by the incident, Martin was electri-fied. For the rest of the walk he kept rummaging around in the undergrowth, hoping to frighten something into the open. When we got back to the house, he was still bubbling with the near miss – if possible even more enthused than myself. For the rest of the weekend he was like an eager spaniel or excited child, looking at his watch and the weather continually.

'It would be brilliant to see him make a kill!' he said, almost pleading with me to arrange such an event. Somehow he seemed to think it in my power. If only it were!

Unfortunately, however, my trips out to the spinney behind the village are proving fruitless. Certainly I still catch the occasional glimpse of a rabbit, but Sioux rarely even sees them, let alone gives chase, not even when I put one up by almost standing on it the other day. It darted away from us and disappeared straight into the wood, giving him no time even to think about pursuit.

According to the experienced Jack, it is vital that hawks be entered as quickly as possible so that the bird gains as much hunting experience as one can cram in before the end of the season. This is easier said than done. He certainly has the flair and desire to hunt at the moment, but the problem is to find rabbits sufficiently far from their burrows to give him a chance. Of course there are alternatives, such as squirrels, rats or moorhens, but sadly these too seem to share a healthy sense of self-preservation. And they would also need to have had a frontal lobotomy not to get out of the way as soon as he comes within earshot, which, even when the wind is favourable, is a good couple of hundred yards away.

These walks do have other compensations, however. This afternoon, for example, a big dog fox came slinking out of the wood in front of me as I neared the end of my circuit. He had been dislodged by the two children who live in a neighbouring house and were chugging around the field on an all-terrain-vehicle – ATV to the cognoscenti. With a sinking feeling I realised that this meant that there are now four village children equipped with these disgusting mobile chain saws. Inevitably they will spend their holidays chugging up and down the fields, churning out noise pollution and exhaust fumes and terrifying the local fauna – to say nothing of the tracks they leave through the soft soil and mud.

The only benefit the racket afforded me was as a distraction, because Sioux shut up for most of the next ten minutes as he concentrated on his surroundings, tuning in first to the whining of the motor, but then switching to the countless small birds that moved nervously up the hedge in front of us. Fortunately, he recognises that anything as small and agile as a blue tit or blackbird is beyond his capabilities. Were he to fly them he could never catch them, but would instead crash fruitlessly into hedgerows, risking damage to his plumage and bruising his confidence.

In any event, I would get no pleasure from depleting the small birds of the area. There is no shortage of them and sparrowhawks already take their toll, but it is not what Sioux is built for. Just as White had acquired a goshawk for its larder-filling abilities, I had also deliberately got a bird which could catch me things to eat.

We might be separated by over half a century, but it seems that the basic appeal in hunting, killing and eating one's own food is just as strong now as it was in White's day. I want to eat what Sioux catches (all right, I admit I wouldn't eat a rat, but I would have a go at moorhen, squirrel and, of course, rabbit).

If only we could find one.

Tuesday 9 February

HUNTING TRIPS WITH the hawk continue to be unsatisfactory. In spite of my efforts, dawn departures seem to be beyond me, although normally I manage to be up and sufficiently compos mentis to leave the cottage by eight. I have abandoned my hopes of finding any rabbits near the house and am now concentrating my efforts on the quarry.

I usually then continue to walk towards the river in the hope of finding the odd moorhen, notwithstanding the end of the moorhen season ten days ago. They are, say the books, about the only feathered quarry within the capabilities of a red tail.

And all the while Sioux is in full voice – 'Eeeeeee! Eeeeee! Eeeeee!' – a cry which has begun to acquire the capacity to hit a particularly ear-penetrating frequency with unerring accuracy. During these trips, as I trudge along, I am taking a calculated risk: that he flies across the river into Cheeseford territory. With the estate's gamekeepers notoriously trigger-happy, were he to fail to return quickly, I would then have to cross it to fetch him and with no bridge for a couple of miles in either direction, this would inevitably mean fording the river. While the weather is mild at the moment, it is too chilly for me to relish the thought. I'm trying to avoid getting too close to the water.

Steering clear of the river did not mean I stayed dry this morning. The ground was waterlogged, to the extent that there were winter ponds around, formed by puddles in hollows in the fields. Half a dozen mallards were paddling on one – but these took to the air while we were far away and anyway, they are too quick to be of interest to Sioux. Instead he divided his time, alternately flying to and from trees and brooding on my fist – 'Eeeeee! Eeeeee! Eeeeee!'

And as I trudged through the mud, every sense straining – even my hearing, which by now can filter out most of the screeches – my heart jumped with every glimpse of a squirrel flitting along the hedgerow, each rabbit jittering in the undergrowth. Jays always scold us instinctively as they catch sight of him and the mallards added to the clamour as they crashed skywards from the dirty black puddles. There were no rabbits to be seen and signs of digging around the holes in the quarry suggested that someone had been ferreting there.

A heavy-booted plod followed as I completed the circuit by trudging back across the ploughed fields to the car with the hawk still screeching in my ear – 'Eeeeee! Eeeeee! Eeeeee!' I could bear it no longer and flung him off towards a tree as soon as I deemed it to be within range. As he landed, I had the frustration of seeing a rabbit jink out from underneath the bare remains of the hedge below. It bobbed across the furrowed mud, slowed down by the rough ground and unhurried by any sense of immediate threat.

Sioux never saw it, having turned back towards me in expectation of a reward. It had been within easy range.

Yet these walks have their compensations. As I squelch through the mud, the tell-tale undulations in the pasture which date it unmistakably as medieval are clearly visible. These are

93

the last physical remains of peasant strip farming. With my own feet chilled to the bone in spite of modern well-made boots, waterproofed with silicon sealants, it occurs to me that life here during the winter must have been very hard in the past. Thanks to one of the fine-print rules of feudalism, each field was divided between the local families and swapping or selling plots was illegal. This meant that no one could claim to be hard done by – they all had a share of each field, good and bad. As a result, for local villagers with their riverside plots, winter must have been a perpetual round of sodden, freezing, feet.

As I can testify even as I write, cold feet rapidly chill the entire body and thus our ancestors must have had continual shivers. The merest hint of hope to lift the gloom would have been that the climate was warmer then – or at least it was until the Reformation – when the Gulf Stream changed direction and the temperature dropped.

Spring is definitely on its way. The birds are singing their hearts out, tuning up for the mating season, and a pair of collared doves were in full-flow in the ash tree at the bottom of the garden this morning – normally a sound that typifies summer. In addition the local jackdaws, jays and magpies seem even more aggressive towards the hawk than usual, anxious to protect their territories from a rival for food and nest sites.

As I tap my days away on the computer, I am aware of watching the season awake. In particular, a fine ring-necked cock pheasant has established a territory in the field immediately behind my computer screen. This morning, as I stared bleakly out of the window, depressing myself with the thought of Easter and the inevitable return to London, I watched it run all the way down to this bottom corner, where a rival was happily feeding, apparently oblivious to his presence. I thought there would be a fight – and was hoping to witness it – but the challenger obviously contented himself merely by inspecting his potential opponent. The interloper had disappeared into the hedge and the other paraded up and down, crowing with short little chuck-chucks. Five minutes later the trespasser reappeared and it was clear that there was a considerable size difference, the invader being probably a yearling while the other was two or three. The smaller seemed defensive although there were no hostilities. He slowly pecked his way to the wall and hopped over. Once out of sight, however, he crowed a couple of times, provoking an immediate response from his rival who strode quickly up to, and over, the wall. His appearance shut up the smaller bird in mid-flow and he then escorted the upstart out of sight, only to reappear on his own just now. The mating season is evidently only beginning – otherwise there would have been more downright aggression with spurs flying and even the occasional death. Pheasants can be very aggressive and I thought of the possibly apocryphal tale of a poacher who used to tether a game cock with metal spurs outside his cottage every spring. He would then dine on the slaughtered pheasants who came to do battle with the interloper, little guessing how weighted the scales were in favour of the cock.

In similar vein, on the other side of the house, jackdaws are busy inspecting their regular site in the hollow ash in the field. The nights are noisy too. Barks ring out across the valley, as the local vixens are courted by dog foxes, an oddly cat-like wailing when the mating actually occurs. There are other barks too – strangely strangled sounds, like a dog with its neck in a snare. These come from the local muntjac – and there are plenty of them. Too-wit too-woos come clearly through the crisp frosty air from the copse at the bottom of the field as tawny owls mark out their patches for the year ahead. They are very territorial, and although mating is still two months away, they have already established squatters' rights in their chosen nest site.

These sights and sounds produce mixed feelings in me. On the one hand it is a delight to be reminded of the proximity of nature, of new life already mustering itself for the year's growth here in the depths of winter, but it is also a reminder that spring is approaching. Easter represents two big deadlines – the end of the flying season as the moult begins and the return to London. My parents have finally decided – quite reasonably – that they want their cottage back. So it looks like a return to the capital for the hot, muggy months.

Five years ago I spent a year in Australia. It was a wonderful experience, but I returned with a sense of relief. One of the things I missed most was seasonal change. The climate down under might be much better than ours in terms of high temperatures and hours of sunlight, but I missed winter breaking suddenly into spring, spring into summer and so on. In Sydney these glide into each other, each shifting imperceptibly into the next. But out here there is a distinct change, one which occurs almost day by day.

It is at its most pronounced at Easter. One morning it is still winter, cold rain lashing the fields, frosts at night and bare branches silhouetted against the sky. But it seems that only a couple of days later this is a thing of the past. The weather warms up suddenly, May blossom appears on the hawthorns and everything turns a lovely rich fertile green. To witness this tremendous force, even in the tamed fields of Oxfordshire, is one of the first great pleasures that the New Year affords. No wonder that our remote ancestors were prepared to offer virgins in its honour, no coincidence that relatively late, Christianity leaped on the same pagan chariot.

I am becoming desperate about Sioux. His moult is on the way and with it the end of the hunting season. I have to get him to notch up at least one more kill by Easter. The problem is that in spite of all my efforts, we have yet to find a clear-cut chance. In desperation I have decided to borrow a ferret to bolt a rabbit for him before it is too late. With a marked absence of suicidal bunnies in the locality, this looks as if it is going to be the only way I can engineer a flight.

Working ferrets and hawks alongside each other is easy say the books, although they warn that at first the partnership can be more than a little risky. If a hawk can cope with a bucking rabbit, then a ferret is well within its capabilities. The trick, apparently, is to put the ferret's cage within sight of the hawk, thus getting it used to the thing: then there

96

should be no problems. I hope they're right: I can't see any ferret owner being pleased to discover that my hawk has killed the pet they loaned me for 'just a couple of days'.

Thursday 11 February

I DROVE INTO Oxford today for the weekly laundry trip and to fetch some necessary parts for the car. Lunch with my mother was followed by shopping and I found myself leaving the city too late to fly the hawk. Instead I returned via a near-by village to pick up a ferret from the man who, fifteen years before, had equipped me with the pets of my youth.

I had driven out there yesterday to inquire about the possibility of borrowing one. In the intervening years, Sean, the ferret keeper, had moved out from the council bungalow that he shared with his parents and brother – most probably evicted by his family because of his twenty or thirty pungent pets. It became clear from the conversation that his remaining relatives don't like ferrets. (Perhaps this is a cross that every owner has to bear?) I persuaded a reluctant brother to give me Sean's number and a call later in the evening revealed that not only could I borrow a ferret, but that I could have one, of any sex or colour. After much debate an albino hob was settled on (or rather 'dog' as they are called around here).

Much as this goes against my sense of the aesthetic, the reasons are sound. Not only are albinos more difficult for the hawk to mistake for a rabbit, but the breeding season is almost upon us. According to legend, bitch ferrets have to be mated or will die (this is based on fact – they ovulate during inter-course and if unmated will remain on heat all summer, which is not good for them). Perhaps unsurprisingly, I think that my livestock needs no further additions right now.

Sure enough, when I pitched up at the door, a white dog was waiting for me.

'There 'e is,' said Sean's brother. 'You go' take 'im out though – Oi don' like 'em. You can 'ave 'im's long as you don' take box.'

Getting him back to the cottage and installing him in his

97

hutch was a simple matter and I still had enough time to take the hawk out for a few minutes, although he was in a foul mood and flew badly in the gathering gloom.

I found loads of messages, including one from a creditor. Much as I increasingly despise the stuff, I have been worried about money recently. In spite of the purifying country air and the absolution for the soul which falconry has increasingly been granting me, no work for the last couple of months has taken its toll. The most terrifying aspect of this has been the thought that I might have to return to London earlier than planned in search of work.

My first reaction to his call was pessimistic. Guessing that he was phoning to tell me I wasn't going to be paid, I rang back with reluctance. He began with pleasantries. His tone immediately showed that clearly he wasn't going to cut my money, but instead was trying to butter me up. He asked after the weather and then – dead giveaway – whether I was overworked.

'Oh it's busy, but not overwhelming,' I lied. Again, like the questions about the weather, this is a necessary formality. No freelance can ever admit to being desperate, any more than an editor can do other than begin by asking how you are, whether your family is well and so on. Editors are always chummy, talking to you as a long lost friend, and freelancers are always busy, just coping with the tide of work that seems to flood in continually.

He finally got to the point. Would I like to write a series of articles for him? ('Hm,' I thought. 'I bet he wants a flattering piece designed to rustle up advertising.')

'You may have seen the magazine and seen how we do regional surveys,' he continued. ('I'm right,' I thought.)

'They're advertising-led, of course,' he said. 'The exact length will depend on how many ads we can get together, but we're thinking of about four or five thousand words. How are you placed for the next couple of weeks or so?'

That made me sit up.

'Where is it?' I asked, checking myself for a moment or two in an attempt to keep the enthusiasm out of my voice.

It was his turn to pause just slightly: 'Um, Lebanon actually,' he said.

Radio 4's *Book at Bedtime* this week has been a serialisation of Brian Keenan's autobiographical account of the five years he spent chained to a radiator in Beirut. Not surprisingly, positive joy was not my first reaction to the news. With £1,000 – £1,500 at stake and no work, however, I was not going to look the proverbial gift horse in the mouth, even if this particular horse looks dangerously Trojan, with God knows what lurking inside.

I accepted, comforting myself that at least the news would produce horror and outrage from assorted friends. I would, if nothing else, emerge as a hero in their eyes.

But no: my girlfriend, Bel, wished she was going (and she's terrified of flying), Charles wanted to know why he never got to go abroad on assignments and if Julie seemed upset it seemed to be only because it meant a planned trip out here at the weekend might have to be cancelled. At least mothers are good for a horrified reaction, I thought, but she was just pleased I'd got some work and told me to make sure I took my camera.

Even my Grandmother merely said 'Gracious!' (While the ferret produced a 'You mustn't!!!!') Was I going mad? 'That's Beirut, Lebanon, Granny,' I said helpfully, thinking that perhaps she hadn't heard me correctly. 'Yes, yes,' she said, perhaps a little impatient at being so patronised. 'They kidnap journalists there,' I said with a vague twinge of desperation. But there was no stirring her.

And in the pub Phil and Mick just thought it the opportunity of a lifetime. Could I take a card? They asked. 'Must be plenty of building work out there,' Mick chortled.

Am I becoming paranoid? My interest in falconry seems to excite more concern among my friends and relations than a trip to a country attempting to patch up the scars of seventeen years of civil war. I can't help feeling a reluctance about going, the more so because although it will save me financially, enabling me to last out here until Easter and the moult, a week in Lebanon will obviously mean giving up hawking for a corresponding period – seven vital days missed.

Saturday 13 February

IT WAS WHILE I was pondering the thought of Beirut that I was bitten by the ferret. He was running around the house, pestered by Havoc who seems to think that he ('Muffin' as Julie has dubbed him) is a beautiful toy, designed solely for her own use. No, bitten is a bit strong: he nipped me, just drawing blood. This was annoying and upset a friend's daughter who was staying for the weekend. She screwed up her face in sympathetic pain and screamed. The sight of the blood, far too bright and glossy to seem real, elicited a Pavlovian reaction in her and I had to point out quickly that it was me, not her, who was bleeding, and that I wasn't crying was I?

Nevertheless, I was bothered by the bite and remembered some advice on how to cure a biting ferret: present it with your knuckle and if it attempts a nip, thrust the bone with its tightly stretched skin down the thing's throat, making the experience as unpleasant as possible. This I did.

The ferret proceeded to chew on the knuckle and I continued to present the thing, time and again to it, pushing my clenched fist into the creature's mouth. After a few minutes it became clear that the process wasn't working very well. Muffin bit with enthusiasm – indeed, as the process went on, he seemed to be keener rather than more reluctant. My fist meanwhile was beginning to drip with blood, the ruby liquid dribbling down the backs of my fingers and splashing on to the floor. I put him away and reflected on this. Beforehand he had been perfectly quiet, now he was anxious to bite. I think my memory had left out some vital part of the advice. As a general rule, kindness and constant handling are the ways to keep a ferret calm.

Biting apart, he is actually quite a nice little creature. Although I much prefer the polecat variety of ferret, with its beautiful brown coat and white mask markings on its face, albinos are *de rigueur* for hawking.

Muffin is unusually small for a dog ferret. Normally males are much, much bigger than their sisters. They can be over two feet long and weigh three to four pounds. Muffin, however, is smaller than most jills; just a foot from nose to tail and tipping the scales at a pound. He is what used to be called a 'greyhound' ferret – a small lithe hunter.

His behaviour has, incidentally, drawn my attention to the compost heap again. As I opened the door to push in a couple of chicks to feed him a couple of days ago, he made a bid for freedom, tumbling out of the open and rustling around on the ground near the bonfire. And then again, yesterday, while I cleaned out his pen he wandered around on the ground, ending up at the rear end of the fireplace. Suddenly only half of him was there, the front end having discovered a hole in the wall abutting the compost heap. I grabbed his rear and returned him to his cage, but then went back to the heap. There seem to be holes in it again. I think these must have been created by the compost subsiding. The tunnels – if that's what they are – are far too large for a mouse and there is nothing else that could have made them.

Monday 15 February

WITH THE ACQUISITION of the ferret, I have to get a move on if I am to use him to bolt rabbits for the hawk. Indeed it might already be too late. It has been such a mild winter that the local rabbits are almost certainly breeding by now. The presence of babies makes ferreting tedious beyond belief as the little hunter kills and eats the kits before falling asleep on their corpses.

I took the opportunity of getting a car service and enlisted the help of Brian to drive us for our attempt, a water bailiff from the Cheeseford Estate, who I got talking to in the pub last week. We drove to the quarry near the river. In theory he was going to handle the ferret, but as we walked towards the rabbit bury, I thought it incumbent on me to warn him that the creature was not absolutely steady. He clearly registered this and confessed to not really liking ferrets although he quickly claimed to have done enough rabbiting in his time. As we strode along, his dog, Dan, bounced around us. He is a bright border collie who has been partially trained in field trial work. Not that Brian uses him on sheep, mind you. Instead Dan spends the spring and summer rounding up pheasants on the estate, driving them in and out of the rearing pens. In the winter he helps beat the woods for the guns that rent a day's shooting.

Brian is a 'foreigner', originating from Nottingham. He moved to the district about two years ago and manages the Cheeseford lakes, stocking them with trout and attempting to keep the pike and coarse fish under control. He also helps out around the estate, culling deer and keeping vigil for poachers.

In many ways we have much in common. We both dislike foxhunting because of the noise and inefficiency (he pointed out that over the last five years the hunt have failed to make one kill on the estate). Like me he would not have it banned, however, his thinking being that as long as it is allowed, activists will concentrate on disrupting it, leaving his own sport alone.

His idea of heaven is to spend the day coarse fishing, sitting quietly on the bank of some canal or pond, catching as many fish as possible, only to weigh and throw them back at the end of the day. I said that although I wouldn't ban it, to me it is the cruellest field sport: driving a barbed hook into the mouth of a creature with a highly developed nervous system, only to rip it out and return the thing to its environment can hardly be described as cruelty-free or purposeful. Brian hadn't considered this, but said in its defence that if it weren't for fishing competitions there wouldn't be any fish in many of Britain's rivers.

'They're good for the fish,' he argued. 'If it weren't for them there wouldn't be any in rivers like the Trent. If you have a competition, with records going back forty years and the combined catch begins to drop, they're the first on to the National Rivers Authority. With five hundred anglers spread over two miles of river and records going back that far, there's no way the NRA can ignore the numbers as unscientific.'

In common with many keepers, Brian is not highly talkative, his conversation sprinkled with sparkling bouts of silence. But as we proceeded, he gradually melted, taking pride in showing Dan drop on command, but admitting ruefully as the dog turned a deaf ear to course two hares half-heartedly across the field, that he could be better. 'But I'm soft on him,' he said, confessing shamefacedly that he is not only allowed to sleep indoors, but on the bed.

Slightly to my surprise, he also turns out to be a very gentle man, a firm believer that a dog must never be hit – or at least that a collie should never be physically chastised. Apparently Dan was part-trained by someone else before being rejected as not good enough. The first owner had struck him frequently, resulting in the dog having a tendency to cower that Brian had yet to eradicate completely. As he mentioned this his brow clouded: 'I wish I could get my hands on that bastard,' he muttered darkly. Coming from a man who earns his living from what field sports proponents call 'control' and anti-blood sports campaigners call 'murdering', this might seem odd, but after living here for the best part of a year or so, there now seems nothing incongruous about this at all. Death in the country is as much a part of life as birth. You accept that the one cannot happen without the other.

If Brian is naturally taciturn, the presence of the hawk is a great ice-breaker. Although he was too heavy to fly well, he did enough to impress the water bailiff, making an attempt at the one rabbit which we bolted. And although he was slow to come out of trees, he was still sufficiently good to show what he might be capable of.

Brian became positively effusive and wanted to get me permission to fly on the Cheeseford estate immediately. Apparently there aren't many rabbits there at the moment – to the extent that they are being afforded semi-protection – but he thought that permission to hunt a few could be easily obtained, particularly as the keepers have just been made redundant and are therefore less possessive than might otherwise have been the case.

The mention of the lay-offs depressed Brian, however. Apparently the running of the estate is about to be changed completely, with the shooting and fishing sub-contracted out to a professional game manager, who in turn will let it out to paying guns. To put this into practice, the four keepers have been fired. Although Brian's own job is comparatively safe, the manner in which his colleagues have been treated clearly upset him. Not only are they friends, but they have been given their cards at the worst time of year for anyone working on the land. He said the atmosphere on the estate is at an all-time low.

After spending my youth here and being raised on the legendary tales of the viciousness of the Cheeseford keepers, of dogs shot on leads, propping nails against the tyres of parked cars and the like, Brian's news strikes an odd note. Many of the stories were appalling, such as the one about a 'transvestite' who was beaten up by the head keeper. The victim turned out to be a local vicar wearing jungle shorts. It may be apocryphal, but at least one story was true, for a few years ago a couple of keepers were prosecuted for planting a pheasant and shotgun on a local plumber driving across the estate. Unfortunately for them, however, it quickly emerged in court that he had never owned a gun and was known as an animal lover. The Cheeseford case collapsed and the keepers ended up with jail sentences themselves. In contrast to these appalling stories, Brian paints a picture of friendly, reasonable men simply getting on with their jobs. As he talked, I began to wonder how true the tales ever were. Rumour can be one of the most effective deterrents to would-be trespassers.

Whatever the truth now, everything is about to change. Currently the estate's keepers rear a large, but reasonable, number of pheasants every year, to be turned free. Their progress is carefully monitored and the birds fed at selected sites, the aim being to produce 'high-quality, high-flying birds', rather than the biggest bags possible. This is all to change apparently, with the emphasis on quantity rather than quality. This, says Brian pessimistically, will result in over-stocking with high mortality through disease and predation. And how, he adds gloomily, can half the number of men be expected to produce twice as many birds?

'By roping me in, that's how!'

Redundancy is a horrible word anywhere, but clearly it has a particular horror in the countryside at the wrong time of year. A keeper looking for work in the spring has as much hope of finding a job as an Ebbw Vale miner finding work in South Wales. The sackings have had a demoralising effect on all the other estate workers, said Brian. This would be bad enough in a factory, but when they regularly put in 80-hour weeks without overtime during the summer out of a genuine love of the job, the effects of depressed morale must be very serious.

In spite of this and the fact that we caught nothing, he was in a good mood and even the first spots of rain did nothing to dampen this. He was all for going there and then to Cheeseford to ask the head keeper for permission to fly and it was only because the hawk was becoming recalcitrant that I declined. This was not really a surprise. Jack reckons that you should fly birds at as heavy a weight as possible. As a result, I have been trying to bring up his weight slightly and now, instead of being 820g, he was 880g this morning.

Although he flew reasonably to begin with, as the morning progressed he became slower and slower, finally refusing to come down from an ash tree for a quarter of an hour. Some of this could be put down to Brian and Dan, both of whom he is unused to, but undoubtedly the weight was an important factor. There was a counterbalancing benefit, however. Having the edge taken off his hunger resulted in a remarkably silent day's hawking. Instead of being on the edge of starvation, he was much more interested in his surroundings. I continue to cherish my hopes that he might shut up for good one day – but when I am being honest with myself, I have to confess this seems unlikely.

Because I am still unsure about his reactions to the ferret, rather than hunting him out of a tree, I decided to have him on my fist, his jesses clenched tightly between my fingers, ready for release only when a rabbit emerged. This was clearly a wise move, for several times he bated towards the ferret, murder in his eyes. The one rabbit that we did flush was out of a rotting pile of old straw. It bounced rapidly across the quarry bottom and I flung the bird after its retreating scut, attempting to build up some sort of impetus. But he was half-hearted about it, probably correctly deducing that he couldn't hope to catch the thing.

So the morning ended with him glowering in the ash tree, rain spitting down on the three of us waiting below, with a kestrel mobbing us from a safe distance. It resented the presence of a potential rival for the local mice and voles. Driving back to the cottage, we continued to chat about the running of the estate. Apparently the use of franchise management is a growing trend, with the farming and fishing – and now shooting – sub-contracted out in return for guaranteed income. The heir to the estate, who now runs it for his father, has no head for farming and is apparently only interested in horse-riding.

A cup of tea later and Brian left, promising to be in touch about the rabbiting. When I said how much I liked venison and pike, he winked and promised to see what he could do. Muntjac were particularly plentiful, he said, the little deer shot around the year in the forest: 'They have to be culled and if someone wants to pay for it, so much the better.'

After he'd gone I rang the garage to find that they'd finished the service. I had to walk in to pick up the car during the afternoon, catching a glimpse of a magnificent sparrowhawk flitting down the hedgerow in front of me. After the disaster of DDT poisoning working its way up the food chain in the Fifties and Sixties, these have recovered in numbers and are now common almost everywhere. But they are difficult to spot, unless you know what to look for. Until a couple of years ago I had hardly ever seen one here, but like so many things, my sightings have now become relatively frequent.

In essence you look for a brown, nondescript bird that shoots along the hedgerow, flying low to the ground, but with more purpose than a thrush or blackbird. Instead of alighting after twenty yards or so, it continues its flight, darting away from the observer. But they are still difficult to see and immature birds are easily mistaken for a female blackbird.

Sure enough this one flitted up the hedgerow as I reached the outskirts of the town, skipping along inches from the ground, but unlike a blackbird it kept going along the hedge and then, rather than flitting into it, the hawk shot across the road into the ivy-covered wall. If there had been any doubt as to its identity, the rapid exodus of pigeons from the dense foliage gave it away. Unfortunately, although I could see it was an immature bird, cloaked in the drab brown of a passager, it was difficult to tell whether it was a musket or spar. The former are tiny in comparison with their sisters, being about the same size if not smaller than a blackbird, while the females are considerably bigger, weighing anything up to twice as much.

The sight reminded me of an incident last August that had been another important factor in persuading me to go ahead with getting a hawk. A former girlfriend, Charlotte, and I were sitting in the garden, lounging in the evening sunlight, about to have a barbecue. My attention kept wandering up the hedgerow, trying to spot the little owl, which was nesting in a tree at the end of the lane. It was normally to be seen around in the early evening, but on this occasion it was nowhere in sight. Instead there were just a couple of blackbirds, one a fledgling, the other an anxious parent trying to teach it to fend for itself. The weather was perfect – warm and hazy at the end of a long day. And then, out of the corner of my eye, I caught sight of a falling grey-brown form, which seemed to plummet from the ash tree. A terrific 'chinking' started up from one of the birds, a plaintive squeaking from the other. Obviously something had just caught the fledgling – the little owl? Unlikely, they are barely bigger than a blackbird and a fully grown youngster would surely be too big for one to manage? The same would go for a kestrel – and anyway, the hunting style was wrong. It had to be a sparrowhawk. It must have flown low and fast along the lane, spotted the two birds through the hawthorn hedge and flipped through the branches, dropping on the youngster, invisible until the last split second.

Notwithstanding the hawk's superior size and power, it still took time for it to deal with the fledgling, even though it was strong enough to pick up the corpse and fly across the hedge into the lane when it realised I was watching it, pulse racing and throat tightened with excitement. I crossed the garden to stare down the lane to where the hawk was mantling over its prey in the dust. They are furtive birds, wary of man after years of persecution and reluctantly I had to leave it to its kill, scared I might frighten it off and, who knows, deprive its youngsters of an evening meal.

The next morning I found a small burst of dark brown feathers to mark the spot. There was no other sign of the incident, the hawk must have managed to carry it off to its nest, wherever that might be. The incident is still etched on my memory and it is one I am privileged to have witnessed. Sparrowhawks are *so* difficult to spot, let alone see hunting.

Tuesday 16 February

I AM STILL waiting to hear whether the trip to Beirut is on. I rang to find out, but the ads still have to be sorted out and everything is uncertain. I am still very much in two minds about the whole thing. On the one hand it is money that I have to have, but on the other it means leaving here just as Sioux needs most time and effort spent on him. Jack's warning to get him killing as quickly as possible to boost his confidence and perhaps shut up his screams, was still ringing in my ears.

After his moody response to Brian and Dan, Sioux is now back on good form, having dropped back to 845g. But there are still precious few rabbits around. Instead, as we strode down the field, round a little copse and up towards the site of the abandoned village, I was struck by the quantity of munjac slots in the mud: two chisel marks that could not possibly be made by or mistaken for anything else.

Brian says they are shot all year round in the forest, having no fixed breeding season, but rather a seven month cycle. They do little damage, but have to be controlled to some extent, lacking any other predators.

'There's no closed season,' he said. 'But you have to shoot the does when they're heavily pregnant, when their current fawn is weaned and ready to fend for itself. If you shoot a doe about to give birth then it's simple and humane.' He also added that muntjac are the best eating deer, and apparently those on the estate are reserved for the big house and not sold. Mind you, he also pointed out that at only a little larger than a hare, there is barely enough meat for six or seven servings on a whole carcass.

A little further on and there was a small puff of rabbit fur. Fox spoor nearby in the form of a cat-sized paw print told the tale, although around here there is precious little else capable of taking rabbits, apart from, conceivably, mink and the occasional stoat or weasel. But none of these are common, although they do exist. Normally I would have noted the signs with interest, but on this occasion it was merely frustrating. There is now one fewer rabbit around for Sioux to catch.

Wednesday 17 February

ONE OF THE most immediate effects of Sioux's arrival was that I virtually abandoned watching television (apart from natural history programmes). Instead I spend my precious daylight hours with the hawk and work during bad weather or after dark. The evenings speed by that way and as a break from the computer screen, I tend to pop into the local town to have a drink at the end of the day. To avoid the danger of inadvertently drink-driving, I go half-an-hour before last orders – that way it is almost impossible to down more than a couple of pints with Phil.

On one such trip I found him propping up the bar in *The King's Head*, accompanied by Mick. My arrival was the excuse to leave the pub – to trot across the road to *The White Hart*. This ritual seems ludicrous, but it is a charade trotted out every night by the pair: and the rest of the town's drinking population for that matter.

It is a pointless exercise as far as any outside observer is concerned. Prices are the same in each pub and the beers much of a muchness. You might think that variations in clientele form the appeal, but as everyone makes the same move, this cannot be the attraction.

The phenomenon is at its most marked on Saturday nights, when at nine everyone in *The King's Head* walks across the road to *The White Hart*. Then, on the dot of 10.30, everyone in *The White Hart* glances at the clock, swills down the dregs of the pints they've been caressing, and walks back across the road to *The King's Head*. On other days of the week the ritual can be varied slightly – maybe an excursion to *The Crown*, or if the drinkers are feeling particularly energetic, a further hundred yards along the road is *The Railway Arms*. The one constant is the finale in *The King's Head*. Old hands like Phil and Mick now have it down to a perfect art – arrive with at least ten minutes left and two or three pints can be squeezed in before time is called.

Phil always swears that he never used to be like this, that he would normally spend three or four nights a week in, and that it's only since Christmas he's been out every night with Mick. The latter, in spite of his apparently boundless good humour and sense of fun, is 'deeply depressed', according to Phil. His wife has been having an affair with a local man: 'I knows him and he's one of them using types – no good at all,' whispered Phil conspiratorially as Mick laughed and chatted to other regulars behind my shoulder. 'Be careful what you say, he gets very depressed easily,' he added.

Looking at Mick as he threw back his head and guffawed, his thin features slightly flushed with the cold of the evening's walk and the effects of six pints of lager, it is difficult to see quite how this could be true. But Phil knows Mick better than I. It is another warning of the contrasts of such a small community with a big city like London. Phil seemed to know everyone in the town – or at least everyone worth knowing.

In *The White Hart* he had whispered to me about the

middle-aged man two seats away from me – 'He's a right pain,' he whispered. 'He was having an affair with the receptionist at the business centre while I was working there – she was married and he got to be a right nuisance, phoning up all the time.' Two seats further on was a farmer who'd once turned nasty over a woman in *The King's Head*, while the woman next to him was Phil's ex-wife's best friend and lived next door to the man who was due to marry her. On the other side of the bar was Mark, about to marry Phil's ex-wife's daughter. As we surveyed the locals, Phil muttering snippets of gossip, most of which seem to revolve around sex in some form or another, I was struck by how similar the town's social life is to the atmosphere of a big mixed boarding school: incestuous and at times claustrophobic.

In contrast, in London or any other big city, if a marriage breaks up, it is normally a quiet process – at least as far as next-door neighbours and friends are concerned. In the anonymity of a crowd, the pain and trauma of divorce and adultery can be hidden from the world. Here they are thrust into the limelight. The adulterer wrecking your marriage is a familiar face. He is the man who stands next to you in the pub every night, the woman who queues behind you in the Co-op or who rummages through the shelves in the library, competing with you for the latest P. D. James. If their identity is known to you, so the opportunities for taking action are restricted. A domestic row in a city street might raise the neighbours' eyebrows, but little more: here a punch-up at the weekend will be common knowledge within minutes, the gossip passed on to shoppers by the butcher, to drinkers by Phil and by a hundred other tongues on the pavement and in the doctor's surgery.

But in the main life is remarkably quiet. Violence in any form is as rare as theft – although burglary is certainly a fact of life on some of the estates on the outskirts of the town and not unknown in tiny hamlets such as mine (five months previously some neighbours came back from the 'school run' and disturbed two men with their valuables packed into pillow cases).

Having said violence is rare, it is not non-existent. Last summer Phil had an argument with Kim, one of the town's two 'bad 'uns'. He and his twin brother Steve are in their early thirties and between them have been banned from every pub for twenty miles in any direction. Steve is less trouble than his brother, merely alcoholic, druggy and incoherent. He is a town nuisance rather than a nightmare. By all accounts his brother is much worse, although I have never met him, because he's been barred from every location where we might cross paths.

He was exiled for good from *The King's Head* following an argument with Phil. Kim had downed a skinful and a row broke out. Not the first time he'd caused trouble, it was the last straw for Tom the landlord. Kim was kicked out, but started a scuffle in the street, and ended up hitting a passing woman. Outraged, Phil, a burly man who must weigh twenty stone, laid him out with one punch. That was that as far as the big builder was concerned.

But Kim apparently did not agree. He brooded on the problem overnight and returned to the centre of the town at six the next morning. Phil's door is always unlocked and the young man, none the wiser for a night sobering up, mounted the stairs to the bedroom at a charge. In his fist was a kitchen knife. Fortunately Phil was woken by the sound of thunderous steps on the stairs and met him, clad only in his underpants on the landing. A scuffle broke out, during which blood – Phil's – was drawn. Not unnaturally the latter lost his temper and ended up chasing Kim down Church Street as dawn broke over the roof of *The Crown*.

Equally predictable was the effect of the noise. Every inhabitant of the centre of the town was woken. It was no surprise that Kim could easily outrun the weighty Phil, although with his blood up in more senses than one, the latter managed to get out of the village before he gave up the chase. He returned to his flat, clad only in a pair of light blue Y-fronts, to find the police waiting and every window in the street opened, with heads hanging out.

Oddly enough, Phil and the police seemed the only ones

not to see the humour of the situation. Aggravated burglary was the charge and Kim seemed certain to face three or four years inside.

The prosecution had to be abandoned and Kim was let off with a caution. The reason? Phil's elderly mother lived next door to Kim's widowed mother. The two women relied on each other for company and help with the shopping when one or the other was laid low with arthritis. Faced with the loss of her son, Kim's parent appealed to her friend and in turn the pressure was put on. Much to Phil's disgust he saw no option but to drop the charges. The mention of Kim's name still brings a curl to his lip: 'It's coming at me when Oi'm sleeping that gets me,' he says in an aggrieved tone. 'Oi mean, it's dangerous innit?' Looking at Phil's considerable frame I am bound to say it seems quite sensible to me – at least it is if Kim is built anything like his diminutive twin brother.

Kim's behaviour seems to have served a useful cathartic purpose for the drinking population of the town. Whenever he feels annoyed or in need of sympathy, Phil need only to raise the matter to excite Tom's interest. Fed up with months of bad behaviour and grateful to Phil for his intercession, the landlord is always quick to seize on the most recent story to filter back, via some errant drinker, of the latest rural pub to bar the tearaway. For Tom such stories are important – they justify his continued refusal to admit the troublemaker. In such a small town it is important to keep in tune with opinion and although Kim is well-liked by the pub clientele when sober, the barring remains popular.

All this is really little more than a minor distraction from my new-found purpose in life. Importantly, Brian phoned up from Cheeseford. He is still keen to go hawking again: and I seem to have enrolled a helper in entering the bird. He has been as good as his word in approaching Johnny, the head keeper. Sure enough he has got me permission to fly the hawk on the other side of the estate on some open downland. There is apparently an old manor house there, surrounded by the remains of a moat which has plenty of rabbits and, better still, no cover nearby. In theory it would be possible to flush rabbits across the open land, giving him a chance of catching them in fair flight. There are also supposed to be a lot down by the railway line. Ferreting here is seemingly impossible, owing to the depth and complexity of the warren. 'Once down it will never come back,' warned Brian. 'But the guy who told me about it said he saw eleven on Monday at midday, so it's obviously not necessary.'

The thought of it is making me almost ecstatic with excitement and I doubt I will be able to sleep tonight. Again and again the old dream keeps returning: the romantic image of snow-covered fields, hawk in flight, while a rabbit tears away towards its bury, puffs of powder snow spraying behind it, my breath clouding in the crisp winter air. I keep praying for snow before the end of the week.

Thursday 18 February

NOW THE HUNT will have to wait. For the time being Lebanon is taking up frustratingly large chunks of my time. Today, for example, I had to drive to London to arrange the details. Not only did I need a good briefing of what has to be done in the Middle East, but a visa has to be arranged. Annoyingly, I still don't know whether the trip is definitely on, but had to risk a totally wasted day on the assumption it would take place. It also risked costing me both of the day's flights with Sioux.

The visit only served to remind me how much I now hate London. Odd really, when only a year ago I was living happily in Islington, congratulating myself on how lucky I was to have a flat there. Now I have a growing certainty that I am going to quit the city for good.

Fortunately for me, work is now looking up on all fronts. As it does every three months when most needed, a civil service magazine has come to the rescue. Aware that it was due soon, I had finally cracked and phoned the editor yesterday to ask whether or not a new issue was imminent. To my relief it is and I hinted very strongly that two, or even three, articles would be more welcome than one. She seemed to take the suggestion and said she'd be in touch soon. The one great thing about this government that I am prepared to concede is that it not only pays well, but almost more importantly, it pays quickly, the result of orders from on high rather than any particular efficiency.

Apparently the government was embarrassed a couple of years ago by allegations that businesses were being forced into bankruptcy by late payment – sometimes from its own departments. It has ruled that the Civil Service must pay within three weeks of receiving an invoice. This contrasts very favourably with the two to three months' delay of my commercial clients.

The complaint is a common one. Phil is similarly afflicted, although as he points out lugubriously, it is more serious for him. His particular problems lie with the insurance companies and builders who sub-contract him. It is he, complains Phil bitterly, who has to pay for materials and pay interest on his bank overdraft. And while his bank manager threatens legal action, he has to watch his clients buying drinks across the bar with the money they owe him.

I managed, somehow, to return in time to fly the hawk before dusk. In contrast to Monday when everything had put him in a bad mood, he was in fine form, being sufficiently keen to eye the neighbour's scotties with more than passing interest. I carried on with him, around the back of a local farm and the adjoining plantation. There were more rabbits than usual in evidence, but all were out of range – and Sioux knew it. This was what Jack had stressed – until he killed something, he would be unwilling to put in the effort.

A vicious circle. Until he tries hard, he is unlikely to catch anything, the local bunnies being sadly all too well-endowed with a sense of self-preservation. In general, however, he is flying well, moving with a sense of urgency and speed, to say nothing of following me well – he really does seem to be learning fast. Oh, if only I could arrange a kill! I'm beginning to wonder if, perhaps, I should be talking to Brian about the possibilities of squirrel hunting?

Mind you, this is a mark of desperation. Squirrels have a nasty bite and have deprived hawks of claws and toes more than once in the past. But I am getting frantic as the days tick away towards the beginning of the moult and am short of opportunities. Grey squirrels are, after all, his natural prey, being part of the staple diet of wild red tails in America. They are easily within his capabilities and as I saw only the other week, he will certainly go for them given the chance.

When I got back from the flight, I rang up Brian. He was still raring to go hawking and suggested a trip for tomorrow.

'Fine,' I said. 'Where shall we meet?'

'I thought we could start near the station,' he said. 'Then if we catch nothing, we can go to the manor.'

'OK, fine,' I said. 'When?'

'Best meet early,' he said. 'Before any commuters are around – how about dawn?'

'Er, I'm not at my best really early,' I said with sinking heart. 'When is dawn exactly?'

'Oh you're all right,' he laughed. 'It's not too bad, in fact it's quite late nowadays – not much before 6.30.'

I tried not to let the involuntary flinch show itself in my voice. 'Oh, that's fine! See you there then!' I can already hear myself beginning to grumble in the cold of early light. And now, as I finish today's entry, for once I have registered what Michael Fish is saying: 'blasts of Arctic air' is how he describes the weather. There is just one consolation, the thought of which makes my heart leap: perhaps this will bring the powder snow hunt that has fuelled my dreams for the last six months.

Friday 19 February

I WOKE ALL too abruptly this morning, jerked awake by the screech of the alarm. It was six and there was a raging gale outside. Unfortunately my dreams of a hunt in the snow were not going to be realised today. Instead the wind howled around the house.

'Thank God!' I thought, staggering to my feet to let the

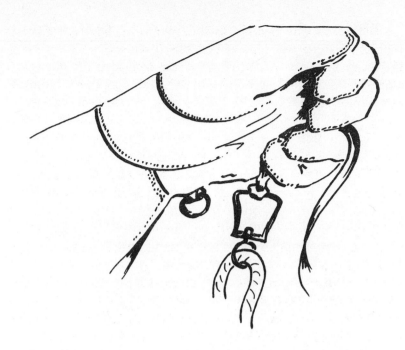

dogs out and make a cup of tea, still bleary-eyed and full of longing for bed. 'Too windy to fly the hawk – we can call off this ghastly idea of meeting at the station.' The image of the hawk, flung by the wind across the river filled my mind's eye. After such undignified flights, he still has a horrible habit of sinking into one of his dark, black, stinking moods, sitting glowering in a tree and ignoring all entreaties to descend. A February wade through waist-deep water is one of those rural experiences I can do without.

Unfortunately, I didn't bank on Brian's enthusiasm. He had left his flat already. Cursing, I pulled on my clothes and gathered up the screeching hawk, who was a little heavier than I'd intended. While driving through the gloom of the approaching dawn, I listened, barely compos mentis, to *Farming Today*, marvelling how anyone could get up this early on a regular basis.

As I parked, the wind seemed to have died almost completely – and any regrets I might have had soon evaporated. Brian was there waiting for me – and had been since about six. He was with Dan, of course, and a .22 rifle. He said there had been half-a-dozen rabbits feeding in the light of the station when he arrived. With his telescopic sight and silencer, he couldn't resist the temptation and had taken a pot shot at one, nominally for food for the hawk. He swore he'd hit it, but there was no sign of the thing when we got to the foot of the slope – nor of any of its relatives. Mind you, there was no shortage of evidence and anyone who disbelieves that rabbits are a pest should take a look at the banks surrounding the station. They were so riddled with holes that they looked like a Swiss cheese in places. The station car park is in serious danger of a landslide into the paddock below.

As I was mentally cursing Brian's trigger-happiness, we walked round the field. There was nothing to be seen. Sioux was in a bad mood, needless to say, perhaps still upset by the presence of a stranger and was slow in and out of the trees, his comparative silence showing that he was not hungry enough. To make matters worse, my nightmare seemed to have come true when one of the rare gusts of wind swept him across the river, leaving him precariously perched above the sewage works. Things worsened when Brian remarked in a blasé voice that there were plenty of rabbits behind the eight foot, razor-wire mounted fence. I had visions of him making his first kill there, leaving me to clamber over the fence while he gorged himself, surrounded by thousands of gallons of effluent, to lumber slowly off the ground, fed up and totally disobedient as I finally staggered up to him.

Luck was on my side, however, and he returned reasonably promptly. Perhaps he was getting used to Brian or was encouraged by the improving light. We then drove up to the lodge whose old moat is supposed to be riddled with rabbits. Again we saw none, but did catch sight of a wild buzzard flying high above us as we drove across the downland – a beautiful, almost black, bird, sprinkled with flecks of white on his neck and wings.

A glance around the surrounding area showed why it was there, of all places. High and windswept, the surrounding fields are open with precious little ground cover and plenty of updrafts for soaring on. Behind lies a piece of ancient woodland, part of the primeval forest that once covered the whole of southern Britain. This would provide plenty of potential nesting-sites and carrion, and, Mark assured me, buzzards are totally unmolested by the keepers (unlike tawny owls which are occasionally shot, illegally, around the pheasant pens if they begin to develop a taste for the poults). It was a magnificent sight, if far too brief, made all the better by still being only the second time I've seen one around here.

We drove back to Brian's flat for a cup of coffee. Shyly he showed me his guns – all four of them – and began to open up conversationally. Familiarity melted his rather gruff manner. He even started to crack a few jokes. As the coffee swilled down, I was beginning to think guiltily of the dogs that by now had been languishing for a couple of hours in the cottage, but Brian was keen to show me the wood. I could hardly refuse, so we hopped on his 'quad', which turned out to be one of the ATVs that I hate so much. Not surprisingly I didn't find it nearly so annoying when I was seated on it, particularly when the physical realisation that I had been up since six began to hit my body.

We shot around his beloved lakes, following the ecstatic Dan who was bounding ahead with the same fervour that Dill or Havoc would have shown, his tongue lolling out, his body tensing and relaxing like a bedspring between the hands of an enthusiastic Slumberland salesman.

There was little to see. A pair of mallards panicked and flew off at our approach; a randy domestic gander that mates, fruitlessly, each year with a Canada goose, waddled to one side; and in the water a dead coot floated. Brian had shot it yesterday. They are not tolerated on the estate because of the danger to ducks. They are such territorial birds that anything invading their territory is attacked. If this happens to be a duckling, the results are usually fatal. He admitted, candidly, that while in general the law was respected on the estate, protected animals such as herons and owls were shot sometimes, but only 'when necessary': theoretically risking massive fines.

'I don't like doing it,' he said. 'Nor shooting foxes,

neither, but when it's your livelihood, you've got to, haven't you?' I kept quiet.

Unfortunately, however, he was unable to show me the forest itself. A party of Danes was shooting there, perched in high seats before dawn by Johnny, the head keeper. 'They're huge and mad that lot,' he said. 'They're dead keen to get muntjac because they don't get them on the Continent and it's another notch on the gun stock, isn't it? They're that trigger-happy that if we surprise them we could end up joining the list.'

I thought of Tom Lehrer's *Hunting Song* (where the narrator describes gleefully how he shot 'four hunters, one game warden and a pure-bred jersey cow'), but again kept my mouth shut.

Finishing the tour, we took the hawk to meet Johnny, the idea being that if I was introduced I could return any time I want to. Unfortunately, however, he was out, fetching the by now frozen Danes from their high seats, to take them back to the local pub to thaw out and swap tales of skill and marksmanship.

His wife, Jenny, and a couple of the other keepers were there, and we went into the house to have a cup of tea. Jenny was very nice – intelligent and caring and not at all like I'd imagined a keeper's wife to be. A motley selection of dogs swirled around the floor, and were kicked out every few minutes, owing to appalling wind problems, only to reappear a few minutes later when the smell was forgotten. Outside the yard was full of chickens, geese and turkeys and the sound of whinnying could be heard from the barn next door, where the estate's owner keeps his horses.

These, apparently, are the only things that interest him. It is clear that it is for this that most of the staff are not over-fond of him. Their attitude seems to be that if only he would pay more attention to the land, to its wildlife and to a land-lord's traditional responsibilities, life would be much better. For example, they are deeply disquieted that he has pulled down many of the old drystone walls around the estate, replacing them with an electric fence, pumped full – incredibly

– with *mains* electricity! Given that the public has right of way to much of the forest, this is, to put it mildly, alarming.

'Would bloody well serve him right if someone with a pacemaker got a jolt,' said Jenny vehemently. 'His insurance company would soon put a stop to it after that.' This is probably true, but it seems a little harsh on some poor innocent with a heart condition.

Her antipathy towards her husband's boss is not so surprising given that they are both about to be thrown out of home and employment, chiefly because he can't be bothered with the estate and is getting someone else to shoulder the responsibility.

Everyone was very interested in the hawk, however, all their eyes lighting up when they saw him. To a proud hawk worshipper, the reaction was satisfying. It also runs totally against my experience when younger of asking permission to go ferreting. Then it was cold stares and polite refusals. In retrospect, my chances of success had not been helped by my youth and the tatty clothes needed for a day which was going (with luck) to be spent grubbing in water-logged ditches and bramble thickets. Nowadays I am more presentable. I also have the self-assurance and accent of a Cambridge education. These things help.

But much more important is the image of the sport itself. There is a tremendous class difference between ferret and hawk. The former, like a lurcher – or 'long dog' as Jenny said with a curl of the lip – has 'disreputable' writ large about it. It is the poacher's (or at best the labourer's) form of hunting. To a keeper, ferrets are at best the smelly things at the bottom of his garden and at worst the mark of a poacher. On the other hand, a hawk is not only associated with aristocracy, of royal hunting trains and mounted falconry expeditions, but its very appearance smacks of *class* with a capital 'C'.

Even better, it seems as if every gamekeeper in Britain dreams of flying one himself: or at least their reactions suggested this. Naturally I was keen to show him off and equally predictably he was anxious to show me up. Off he flapped into a huge beech by the house, to sit and glower, unmoved by my embarrassed entreaties below. Fortunately, however, these are people well-used to animals, rather than town dwellers raised on push-button entertainment. Without being asked they retreated a decent distance and his screams duly changed, to the tell-tale softer chortle that signifies he's on his way. By this stage the crowd had grown, however, with the two grooms from the stables next door coming out to watch, joining the three keepers and Jenny. They were every bit as interested, but of course this merely added to my embarrassment.

I still don't understand how he does it, but he seems to have an unerring sense of the precise moment which will inflict maximum humiliation. Here was I trying to impress someone who could give me permission to hunt over a vast range of land and the bloody bird shows itself to be not merely harmless, but disobedient too.

Wednesday 24 February

I WAS ON my way to his mews to take him out for his early morning flight when I noticed a stirring in the compost heap, a flicker of grey and brown flitting across the corner of my vision. I started and turned, glimpsing a large tail whipping down one of the suspicious holes I'd noticed in the decaying vegetation, dusted with a light hoar frost. A rat.

The sight stopped me abruptly in my tracks, before I realised that there was little I could do immediately. Sioux was screaming at me in anticipation of the exercise and food and I was at a loss for action. So I continued with my hunting trip, but it was not a success, probably, I suspect, because my mind was on the rat and my distracted air conveyed itself to the screaming bundle of feathers on my fist.

I hate rats, loath them. To call this a phobia would be a ludicrous exaggeration. A phobia, as I understand it, is an irrational fear and my distrust of rats is not irrational. Until I got ferrets they didn't bother me in the slightest – no more than any wild animal with a healthy set of teeth might. But when I got my first ferret and began to search avidly for literature on the subject (no mean task for anyone, let alone a twelve-year-old), I discovered what dangerous creatures they are. Apparently, said the books, 55 per cent of rats carry leptospirosis or Weil's disease, a particularly unpleasant form of jaundice (the Victorians knew about the link when they called it 'rat catcher's yellows'). Not only this, rats don't have a sphincter valve. As a result they trail a dribble of urine everywhere they go and it's this which carries the virus. In consequence merely touching somewhere that a rat has scuttled could be deadly.

The general advice amongst ferret pundits on ratting with your pets was 'Don't', and one even accompanied his warning with an anecdote of a banker he'd known who'd asked to go ferreting rabbits as something he'd never done before. During the hunt a rat, accidentally dislodged from a bury, nipped him. 'He was dead within the week!' said the author, with gloomy satisfaction.

Now this got me, an impressionable teenager, thinking. The sort of people who write ferreting books tend not to be the wimpy type. If the best of Britain's ferreters – God, what a vision that conjures up! – are afraid of these little brown creatures, what should I, an adolescent tyro hunter, feel about them? As a result the seed of a very rational dislike was fostered. Not a phobia, but rather an informed, rational, acute awareness of the danger that they represent. Mice I can take, but not rats.

By the time I returned to the cottage I knew what I was going to do. Somewhere, buried in the depths of one of the sheds, was a Fenn trap. Vicious in the power of its jaws, this was the machine that replaced the infamous 'gin trap' of the last century. Unlike its predecessor which was designed to grab and hold whatever triggered it – normally a leg – Fenns are meant to kill. As a result the spring is more powerful and the jaws bigger, made to snap together in an upwards lunge that is quicker than the human eye can follow.

I had found it while trespassing as a child. They were not hard to spot once you knew what to look for: a wooden tunnel at the corner of a wood, in the middle of which lurked the trap. In a fit of compassion for the 'vermin', at first I set off all those I could find. Later I began to remove them so they could not be used. I threw most in a ditch, but brought one home, God knows why. It had lain in the shed, rusting in the damp air, hidden by garden furniture and some tins of coagulated paint.

I set it in the bottom of the bonfire, sprinkling black, damp, ash over the trigger-plate. A dusting of bran flakes baited the thing and, after putting a cover over it to keep out dogs and foxes, I retreated. The next day seemed an eternity. I checked the thing every couple of hours of so, but it was not until yesterday afternoon that I found the thing had been triggered. A half-grown rat – I would say about six weeks old – was hanging from its jaws. It was either too light for the trap or the spring had been weakened by age, and, as the metal jaws snapped together, it had been flung upwards, caught by a leg and its tail.

It hung there quietly until it knew I had spotted it. As I removed the covering, a horrible squealing ensued: a cry of pain and sheer, blind terror, rolled into one. Any elation at the success was immediately quelled by the continuous screams. No one, not even I, with my fear and loathing for its kind, could remain impassive. I ran inside to fetch my ancient airgun, but found that I had no pellets.

Luckily my glove was just inside the kitchen door. With it placed securely on my left hand and screwing my fears down as tightly as I could, I reached down to grasp the trap. I meant to swing it against the wall of the bonfire, but as I picked up the rusty metal, the rat's head swung around and fastened its teeth in the leather.

It is a well-made glove, fortunately, hand-stitched out of doubled buckskin, impervious to even the paralysing grip of a red tail. The rat's teeth, powered by unadulterated terror and pain, locked in the leather, but failed to penetrate it. Everything seemed to be in slow motion, but with that ghastly hold of detail you retain at moments of extreme stress, I noticed a fraction of an inch of the long yellowed enamel of his teeth just showing between his lips and the brown leather.

I was left with a serious problem. It was no longer possible to swing the creature against the fireplace wall – or at least if I made the slightest mistake, I would be in danger of breaking my arm. As I stood there, staring at the creature, I could feel my fear of Wiels disease welling up, simultaneously tightening and drying my throat – if further constriction was possible. There I was with a badly wounded rat fastened to my hand, in danger of going into a hysterical fit and with no help available.

Sioux screeched and, for once, I blessed him for it. He was hungry and suddenly I needed him more than he needed me. Rat swinging from the glove I sidled to the door of his enclosure and entered. He glared at me, head tilted on one side, looking for the offering in my hand. Instead all he spotted was a strange brown furry thing, dangling and swinging naturally with my movement. For a dreadful moment I thought nothing was going to happen, that he didn't – or couldn't – see this odd mixture of hair and metal as food.

I moved the glove in front of his midriff.

I didn't see what happened next, but a foot was suddenly embedded in the rat, his claws sinking into the creature's body, squeezing into invisibility, hidden by that horrible lice-, flea- and mange-infested hair. It gave another squeal and then a terrible wheezing sound, the gasp of a tiny concertina collapsing in a corner.

Mercifully, with a last shuddering convulsion, the rat let go of the glove, presumably intent on transferring the two yellow chisels, the crack between the two outlined with a dribble of blood, into the scaled toes that gripped his chest. But even had it had the energy, there was no chance – Sioux's grip was immovably fastened in his shoulders and neck. The same paralysing pressure that had caused me so much agony the previous December, now transferred to this pathetic six inch body.

With the by now inanimate creature locked in his grip, Sioux transferred his bile to me. He was mantling over rat and trap, feathers fluffed up, beak gaping half open and a furious, continuous, scream came rasping out of him. It took some time – and not a little risk to my unprotected hand – to separate the trap from what was now Sioux's meal. I retreated, very shaken to the kitchen.

I don't normally drink before six on a workday evening, but it was with no guilt whatsoever that I downed a very large whisky immediately afterwards, followed by a second. It was barely past breakfast.

I emerged to see Sioux still hunched over the body, wings umbrellaed over the remains of the cadaver. He had plucked it and little but the skin and tail remained. Spurred on by my presence, he redoubled his attack on the corpse, presumably fearful I might take it away from him. As I watched with morbid fascination and still feeling definitely shaken, the last of the rat disappeared, although the tail remained draped out of the corner of his mouth, like a rakish cigar, for what seemed like an eternity. His crop, normally invisible even after receiving a full day's rations, was swollen to huge proportions. To my drunken eye, it seemed as large as a grapefruit.

Best of all, and in a strange way making the terror and adrenalin of the whole incident worthwhile, he was gloriously quiet – or rather his voice had changed. Perhaps it was my imagination, but there seemed to be a new note in it – a squeak. It was almost as if the rat had achieved a strange form of immortality. Rat-replete and whisky-drenched, it was clearly going to be a wasted day for both of us.

Tuesday 9 March

THE BEIRUT TRIP went well from a work point of view, but was still highly frustrating. Just as spring was beginning to break in the Oxfordshire countryside and Sioux getting to the point where he should be hunted daily, I found myself stuck in a bomb site. It was much less badly damaged than I had imagined, but I was staying in muslim West Beirut, three days into Ramadan. Nightlife was thin on the ground, more, I suspect, from the after-effects of war than for religious reasons. Although the people were very nice and the city's prospects good, I had no desire to stay there beyond the first couple of days, finding myself longing for the green of fields and the company of the dogs. I even missed the scream of the hawk, for God's sake!

My return was delayed however. Instead of the seven days planned (and five I'd hoped for), it was eight days before I eventually got back. And how slowly the time passed. Sioux and the dogs had stayed in London with the long-suffering Vaughan. Fortunately she likes them and has a respect for the hawk – although she baulks at feeding him day-old chicks – but she is still prepared to drop bits of steak into his pen.

I returned to find all was well, in spite of my pessimistic visions of a hawk dangling upside down, with which I had been whiling away the time. Muffin was in similarly fine condition when I went to fetch him from Jenny and Johnny. A trainee keeper had, it turned out, taken quite a shine to him.

I arranged to return on the Sunday to fly the hawk at the Cheeseford rabbits and maybe to buy a deer from the keeper's freezer, but in the event Sioux was still out of sorts after his trip to London, weighing in at well over two pounds, and was certain to misbehave. Anyway, Johnny was not there and only Jenny was present, packing disconsolately, although they are not due to be evicted until next month.

We began to discuss their plight, an opportunity to find out how she really felt about the situation. Obviously she is furious, but is almost angered more – if that is possible – by Johnny's tendency to forgive his boss. Not only are they being turfed out after ten years without so much as an apology, but the way it has been done seems particularly appalling. Without mentioning it to the four keepers, Robert took out an advertisement in *Shooting Times*. This was published on a shoot day, with the result that everyone knew that the four had lost their jobs apart from the men themselves: naturally they had been too busy organising the drives to have had a chance to look at the magazine.

She was annoyed too about the way in which the estate was now to be managed, with as many pheasants as possible pumped on to the land – twice the number already there was the intention. This would inevitably lead to overgrazing, scratched bare earth and parasites. She said the man who was coming to do this was already having trouble on this front at his present Gloucestershire estate, and was forced to call in the Game Conservancy to deal with the disease that was ravaging his stock.

She went on to tell me more about Robert. Her general objection is that he's no 'gentleman'. By this she clearly means the old-fashioned Tory squire, one who might pay poor wages, but compensates this with a sense of non-fiscal values, such as loyalty and duty towards those in his employ. Robert, she said, had none of these virtues. Not only were his wages low, but he seemed determined to try to screw as much out of the estate as possible for the minimum input. For example he had attempted to evict the old lady in the cottage at the end of the lane by burning manure from the stable next door under her window. That began two years ago and the unfortunate woman had complained to the Council. An order was served, commanding him to stop. Reluctantly he complied, but only with the letter, not the spirit, of the law. Now he is stacking the raw manure next to another of her walls, allowing its effluent to ooze out slowly around her house, its smell pervading everything. She is doggedly hanging on, determined to resist his whims (no one knows why he wants her to leave) and Jenny wishes her luck. For her and Johnny there is no such hope of revenge. They will have to go wherever the work is – if a post exists, that is.

There is nothing on the horizon. An interview in Shropshire – for which Johnny was over-qualified – failed to produce work and they are now having to quit a house where they have lived happily for ten years. They have nowhere to go and nothing to do. All things considered, she is remarkably calm about the situation, although the mention of Robert's name brought a cloud to her brow. The fact that he is full of public school charm and has persuaded Johnny that 'he's all right really', is particularly galling to her.

'Can you imagine that?' she said, puffing up with fury.

'He's doing this to us and Johnny just says he's got to earn a living too and has to do what he has to do!' Her voice rose in indignation and her not inconsiderable frame was swollen with anger. I couldn't help thinking that she looked like the hawk in one of his towering rages, feathers fluffing up into a crest, a semaphore message of discontent flaring on the back of his head.

I left, depressed. I had returned from Beirut laden with work. Not only was the piece wanted almost immediately – I had to write three big articles in two days – but the answering machine was laden with messages, including a couple of commissions. 'Twas ever thus – February without work, followed by a hectic March. Nevertheless the work is welcome, with the money running out. This hasn't helped my sense of frustration, however – after the eight hectic days spent in the dust and grime of a Lebanon still wrecked by the traces of war, I want to enjoy the countryside.

Much the most important message was the letter from the trustees of the local estate which has arrived at last. It gives me permission to fly the hawk in selected spots on the periphery of the estate. Although pheasants are no longer reared there, Chris is anxious that the wild ones should not be disturbed. There will be fewer of the birds on the outskirts, and presumably he reckons that if anything, I will frighten them back into the heart of the estate.

Although I've had little chance to see Chris immediately on my return, after a week I had lightened the load sufficiently to look round the patches I am allowed to hunt. He is slight in build, his cheeks flushed with the tell-tale burst veins that show him to have lived a life in the open – a network of mulberry-coloured lines blotching his face, a satellite picture etched in blood. He was flat-capped, his face warmed by a half smile and he was accompanied by Stuart, another estate worker whose precise role was never really explained.

I took the hawk to show him off, but unfortunately yet again I couldn't fly him because his weight, which, in the absence of daily weighing and precise monitoring of his food intake, had crept up while I was away. They looked at him with interest, however, and we drove around the outskirts of the estate, covering three main areas, the two furthest being three miles apart. The most promising spot was the one he'd mentioned on the outskirts of town. Sure enough, close inspection showed the ground to be riddled with holes. Chris's brow furrowed as he stared at the damage.

'Worse'n Oi thought,' he muttered and looked meaningfully at Stuart. The other nodded, but pointed out that shooting was impossible. I was puzzled, but it turns out that the standard way of controlling rabbits on the estate is from the back of a pick-up truck, balancing precariously as it bucks and sways across the fields and taking pot-shots at the creatures as they stare, dazzled, into the headlights. In this case the field is far too steep for a car – trying it would be liable to take a higher toll of humans than bunnies. The alternative – gassing – is impossible with at least two badger sets present in the mass of burrows. Unlike Cheeseford, the local estate is scrupulous in its respect for the law.

As we finished Chris pointed out that someone else owned the adjoining fields and suggested that we call in there on the way back.

'Graham's a noice chap,' he said. 'He'll let you on his land Oi should think.'

It was easily done. As we pulled up the two estate workers were caught by the sight of an old motorbike, worth, the farmer later assured us, £9,000. He had come around the house as we arrived, but didn't see Chris or Stuart who had thrust their heads into the kitchen window and were talking to his wife.

'Can I help you?' Graham had a high, squeaky voice. This, it turns out, is his normal tone. Later Phil and Mick assured me that for years people were convinced he had met with an unfortunate early accident – until, that is, he produced two sons and three daughters.

His farm is small, surrounded on three sides by the estate and on the other by the main road. Nowadays he does little farming, earning money instead from bed and breakfast, selling gas and tree-planting subsidies. He asked me who I was and then gave a smile of recognition when I told him. He had brought down his bulldozer when my parents bought the cottage and helped build the gardens.

I had no idea it was he who had driven the monstrous machine – my earliest memory. It had been the summer of '66. I was two-and-a-half. I remember little of the excursion, naturally, but the point where I was lifted on to the bulldozer's cast iron seat, to grasp the wheel enthusiastically and stare across the valley, thoughts of destruction filling my mind, is still vivid.

When we bought it, the cottage had just been converted from a delightfully run-down affair into something fit for the population of Wilson's 'white heat' generation. It had been 'improved' by one of the typical British builders that have systematically built unimaginative monstrosities across the country and ruined ancient buildings with their profitable 'modernisations'. The bread oven had been knocked down, the chimney and beams boarded up. The deep old enamelled sink had been ripped out of the kitchen, while lino and formica took the place of quarry tiles.

I remember fondly the enthusiasm with which we ripped open the chimney after finding a fallen branch too tempting to ignore. On lighting a fire, the cottage immediately filled with dense choking smoke, forcing us into the kitchen, while Dad floundered around attempting, vainly, to quell the clouds billowing out into the room. He didn't succeed then – and still hasn't – but it opened up a whole new side to the place: of collecting and cutting fuel and the deep, rich, pervasive smell of woodsmoke that has now 'become' the cottage in winter.

Equally significant was the downfall of the ghastly fibre-board ceiling. The builder had put this into the place in a vain attempt to smooth out the offensive irregularities of the oak beams supporting the first floor. It was a desperate attempt to make a seventeenth-century cottage as neat and geometric as a post-war ideal home should be.

The best improvements we – and by that I mean my father – have ever made here were ripping out, roughing up and destroying. The bulldozer heralded the first onslaught. The blade tore through the ground, exposing and crushing worms, insects and toads, its tracks squeezing the air and life out of the soil. From grass and weeds it made bare earth, a building site from the scrappy patch of land. Yet today, a generation later, it is a charming garden, too weedy to be really picturesque or twee, but with a lush green lawn and panoramic views across the valley.

And here was the driver of the bulldozer, squeaking at me in his falsetto. He readily gave me permission to fly my hawk on his land – although he said there were few rabbits on his patch. After seeing the damage to the nearby hedge, I couldn't help thinking that, given the season, there soon would be – unless Chris hits them with something like a nuclear bomb.

Spring is now here. A week ago I saw my first peacock butterfly, looking ragged in the sunlight as it basked on the warm tar of the road, attempting to get its body temperature up enough to look for a mate. Further on, two cock blackbirds were squabbling in the dust of the lane, too busy fighting to pay any attention to my presence, and the next morning I accidentally stepped on two worms, coupling in the dew of early morning. They unfastened rapidly and slid in an instant into the soil – an undignified end to their mating.

They were lucky. I could have been one of the myriad of toads that are now apparent. At night the road at the bottom of the hill is covered with them: a host of the little creatures sitting on the tar, motionless in the headlights. Whether they are on their way to the nearby pond or hoping to catch the first insects of the year as they hover above the warmth of the metalling is unclear. Already, however, several are paired up, the smaller males riding piggy-back on the females, sometimes with a jockey of their own as a confused male, driven mad by the itching of his loins, makes do with what he can get.

After touring my new hunting grounds, feeling by now like some sort of feudal lord, master of all I surveyed, I phoned Jack again. He was, as always, charming, and we talked for ages about falcony and hunting generally. He too had heard about events at Cheeseford and disapproved strongly. Coincidentally, a friend of his works for the Game Conservancy and could corroborate the stories of over-stocking. It is a terrible mess apparently, producing birds riddled with disease and ugly, over-scraped land, more reminiscent of a chicken run than woodland. With the priority given solely to numbers of birds shot, pheasants are reared in huge pens, and only turned loose when needed. The result is bemused, half-tame, birds, which fly low and are pathetically easy targets: 'What they don't realize is that it isn't what people want,' he said. 'I don't enjoy shooting personally, but any shot will tell you there's no fun bagging birds you could knock down with a stick.'

I also told him (slightly shamefaced) about the rat. He laughed: 'If the truth be known, I had a similar experience,' he said. 'Rats are such nasty creatures it's sometimes difficult to know quite how to deal with one of the little buggers who's live and kicking. My gos is as good a way of killing them as any.'

The real reason I had rung him up was to ask his advice. Having flown Sioux after rabbits – even though I'd had no real success – I know I am hooked. The problem is that there are only two chances to fly him each day – morning and evening. At most that means a couple of hours of flying before he has had his day's rations.

The only way to get in more flying is to acquire another bird. I have been thinking of a second red tail – a female this time – which eventually I could pair up with Sioux and breed from. But Jack strongly advised against a second buzzard.

'It would be a great mistake,' he said. 'Red tails are such lazy birds that they need as much exercise and effort as possible. Have two and at best you'll end up with two half-fit hawks, neither of which will perform very well. But more likely one will be better than the other. Then you'd need to be superhuman not to spend more and more time with that one. The gap will grow and you'll end up with one disappointing hawk which you don't like and one good bird which would be even better if only you spent the time on it that you're wasting on the other.' In addition, he pointed out, if I had an imprint, then breeding would probably be impossible. In any event it was a difficult and frustrating activity. He'd only begun because after thirty years of hawking, it was the one thing he hadn't done.

As an alternative I've also been toying with the idea of a falcon and I mentioned this. The plan would be to fly it to the lure rather than hunt it, seeing it stoop and tumble in a manner completely different from Sioux's laboured flight.

He seemed distinctly unimpressed by the mention of the lure. 'Why bother?' he said. 'You've got some big fields near you. If you fly it at rooks you'll have much more fun and a better flying display.' I remembered that he is a falconry purist and considers anything other than hunting a waste of time. I felt slightly ashamed and embarrassed at even having allowed the thought to cross my mind, let alone voice it to him, but the thought of the crows had triggered his attention.

'Well if you're interested, you must come over and see my eyasses in the spring.' He added as an afterthought: 'They've laid five eggs and I candled them yesterday – they're all fertile. Come over and see them at the end of April if you remember.'

If I remember! What a ridiculous idea! My heart is leaping at the prospect. In addition, I think I detect the glimmer of an idea crossing his mind. I know that he doesn't sell the birds he breeds, so perhaps he is considering giving me one? I am not sure, but can't help hoping. His birds, and his peregrines in particular, are so beautiful . . . Dream on, Daniel! Dream on!

Meanwhile the quest for more territory to hunt over has led to other discoveries too. While attempting to enlarge my patch still further, I went along to a scrappy farmyard a couple of hundred yards out of the town. A man was working on a winnowing machine linked, precariously, to a chugging tractor. It was the local postman, his rollie stuck, as always, to his lips. No, the fields were not his, he said, adding that his land straggled around the quarry on the other side of the road.

It contained no rabbits. Anyway, he muttered, the cigarette shaking between his lips, he only had forty acres: 'Can't make livin' out o' 'em,' he grumbled. 'Why else you reck'n Oi'm workin' for Post Office?'

The only small-holding farmer left in the area, he was listening gloomily to the Budget as a light drizzle fell. He shook his head as the Chancellor announced the latest petrol rises. He couldn't understand it. They wanted to curb inflation, yet they were lifting fuel prices. That was bound to raise the cost of transport, which in turn would make food more expensive, wouldn't it? But then again, he said he wasn't sure where inflation actually came in: 'They say Oi muz be makin' a mint ow o' barley,' he pondered lugubriously. 'But brewers are still payin' me £115 a tonne – that's same as ten year gone!' He shook his head again, but his massive frame – almost as broad as its six foot height – showed little sign of deprivation.

Thursday 11 March

I CONTINUE TO BE worried by the healthy state of the compost heap's rat population. I had half-hoped that the youngster in the trap had been a one-off, a young buck driven out from a warren in nearby farm buildings. It was a ludicrous hope of course, dispelled when I saw a grey half-grown baby disappearing into the grass cuttings the other morning.

'If you see one rat there are nine others out of sight,' said Brian with relish when I told him in the pub. 'They don't hang out on their own, they're social animals that live in family groups.' He advised poison, but I said I didn't like the stuff, particularly with dogs and a hawk around.

'Well,' he said with a broad grin, 'You've got a problem then.'

I certainly have. His advice was seconded by Chris and Jack. 'You can try shooting and trapping and will get a few that way,' said the former. 'But you'll never get the adults – they're too wise for that.'

The next few days have proved them right. By sprinkling

bran flakes on to the surface of the heap I coaxed several of the beasts out. I managed, somehow, to shoot three with my ancient, bent-barrelled airgun and caught another four in the Fenn trap, but still the bait disappeared, frequently from the pressure plates of the traps. My efforts seem to have barely dented their numbers.

Reluctantly, I am now considering turning to poison. I hate the stuff for its indiscriminate killing ability and the stench produced by a slowly rotting rat. This can be considerable, as the interior of Sioux's moulting pen gives testimony, its sides flecked with discarded entrails.

But the biggest problem of all from my point of view is that a poisoned and dying rat becomes groggy and wanders around in a drugged and dopey state. Given that at least some of them seem to be living in the wall of the hawk's enclosure and that he knows all about their edible qualities, I didn't need to let my imagination run riot to see the dangers.

As I struggle with the problem of how to exterminate the creatures, I can't help finding the situation ironic. The rats are attracted mainly by the compost heap's warmth and the daily covering of food scraps that I, in my desire to be a good 'green' have been tipping over the surface, but the hawk is another attraction for them. His pen is scattered with food scraps and I am fairly sure that they are foraging over the floor after dark. It is odd to think that during the Middle Ages moulting hawks were in great demand from farmers. They were turned loose in grain stores for the months of indolence, free to fly around the barn and, with luck, keep the vermin under some measure of control.

I mentioned the problem to a friend of Jack's and he laughed.

'I've got a few,' he said. 'Can't stand 'em, but I've learned to live with them provided they stay clear of the house. They hang around my breeding pens and it's surprising how often one looks in to see one of the gosses looking smug with a crop the size of an orange.'

This is easy for him to say. He doesn't 'have a thing about

rats' as I do – nor is it his parents' house that he's living in on trust.

This is all very time consuming, but it is as naught to my main problem – how to enter Sioux successfully. The need to get him killing has become all-important again, now that the aftermath of the Beirut trip has subsided. The problem remains to engineer a situation sufficiently to Sioux's advantage so that he can succeed in catching a rabbit.

I can't help thinking it would be very much easier were I in America or Europe. There the use of bagged quarry is not only legal, but positively encouraged by the experts. If you want to get your peregrine killing, you need a good stock of pigeons, advises Beebe. Put a couple in your hawking bag and toss them out at the appropriate moment, when the hawk is in the best possible position. The falcon will kill the dove and its confidence levels will rise beyond all recognition.

And the use of bagged quarry, such as pheasants or quail, allows foreign falconers to set up hawking competitions, where their birds can be 'served' with identical opportunities and judged for style and efficiency.

This avenue is not open to me. Releasing quarry for anything, animal or human, to kill there and then is illegal (as opposed to rearing pheasants to be shot later which isn't). 'Good sportsmanship' lies behind this fastidiousness. Most creatures are only capable of resolute action when on their home territory. A cunning old buck rabbit which is never more than a few bounds from its bury, one that has stood the test of fox, stoat, ferret and gun, fought off rivals and fathered many litters – he will become as helpless as a new-born kit if put in the middle of a strange field. The same is true for birds – if a trifle less pronounced. Set free in a place unknown to them, they will waste time orienting themselves, looking for the best cover, checking that they don't run slap bang into another, more deadly predator.

In consequence the hunter trying to enter his dog or hawk knows that not only can he engineer the perfect opportunity for his animal to kill, but that the quarry will be disadvantaged. Success is easy to arrange, the killer's morale is boosted and its appetite for destruction whetted. Although this short-cut is not open to the British hunter, I could easily do it. Illegal or not, it would be a simple matter to bolt a rabbit with the ferret, catch it live in a purse net and smuggle it home in a sack. If I then released it at dawn in front of the screaming hawk – no one would be any the wiser.

All the same I wouldn't do it. First, it gets the sport a bad name and could give succour to those that would ban it. I feel myself to be a custodian of the art, not an owner. It is mine on trust and to break the law would harm my fellow falconers. Much more important, however, it is a shortcut, the easy way to success. In spite of my desperate desire to get a kill under Sioux's belt to boost his confidence, I want to do things properly – to have the satisfaction of training him all the way through. And anyway, the primary pleasure of flying a hawk is not to kill, but to watch the flight. There would be no pleasure in a bagged rabbit, even were it to transform him overnight into a successful hunter. From then on it would, in its own way, detract from every future flight. I would feel I had cheated, grown impatient with Sioux and elbowed him onwards, tipping the scales against the rabbit.

Yet it seems an age since Jack told me to get a kill or two notched up as quickly as possible. This would improve him no end, he had said and might – just might – stop his dreadful screaming. The importance of this last factor is sufficient to be whittling away at the edges of my resolve. I can't help thinking how much more pleasant our flying sessions would be if . . . But no, I have my principles to uphold.

The only way to engineer a situation to his advantage is with the alarm clock. I will force myself to get up at dawn tomorrow.

Friday 12 March

FUELLED by this resolution, not only did I wake up early this morning, but I actually pulled myself out of bed. I was determined to catch rabbits and here we were, at the end of the winter, with virtually none to be seen. I could only dream of the hundreds I'd seen in broad daylight the previous summer. I didn't set the clock, but for some reason woke naturally at six as the sun lightened the horizon. Normally I would simply roll over and go back to sleep, but perhaps because of the encouraging conversation with Jack, I got up and let the dogs out. I tipped myself into my jeans and mumbling gently to myself, dismembered a handful of chicks.

It was a slow drive, frost misting the windscreen, and the car's heating system seemed incapable of coping with the ice which crusted the glass. I pulled up on the outskirts of the town and took the screaming bird out of the boot. I walked slowly up the field, my boots brushing through frost that was beginning to melt in the yellow light of dawn, leaving the silhouette of the hedge etched on the grass in a myriad of crystals.

Although the sunlight felt warm it was still cold enough for my eyes to fill with tears in the slight breeze. It was difficult to make out the difference between tussocks and occasional pieces of litter. Every shadow, each darkening of the grass seemed to be a rabbit lying there, a sacrificial lamb, if only Sioux could see it. To my right the sun was rising, swollen and the colour of a blood orange. Blackbirds chinked in alarm among the brambles and tits flitted along the hedge ahead with their peculiar bouncing flight. As is normally the case, once I was striding along, surrounded by the sounds of early spring, I had no regrets about the expedition and thoughts of an early return to bed began to fade.

There were certainly plenty of rabbits around, although quite how many didn't become immediately apparent. A couple were running in circles at the bottom of the dip, gambolling in the best Disney tradition. Fully grown, they seemed prompted purely by the joys of the season. Sioux could see them – I know there's nothing wrong with his sight – but chose to ignore them. He was, I suspect, a little too heavy, and in consequence, inclined to laziness. Instead he flapped into the nearest bush rather than the trees above the bunnies where he would have been perfectly positioned.

I walked on, watching the twitching of brambles, the

white flash of a tail, the motionless silhouette of a pair of ears against the sky on the bank above me. And Sioux was statuesque. The only indication that he had the slightest interest was the occasional, blissful burst of silence. We continued up the field, still catching frequent glimpses of disappearing scuts, but with the hawk lagging behind me there was no hope of a kill.

As I neared the bottom of Graham's field I had a brief moment of panic. I had been too lazy to change his jesses to the holeless field type, thinking that it was unnecessary. After

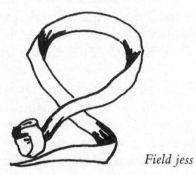

Field jess

all, I reasoned, how often did he get caught up? But he did – amid a chaos of hawthorn branches, about ten feet above the ground and well out of reach. Fortunately by now he was warming up (against all the advice of experts he seems to get keener rather than slower as flying sessions progress) and, after two or three attempts, he managed to pull himself clear, ruffling feathers, but little else. I changed his jesses to the slitless type quickly. Rather forlornly I began to trudge back, thinking it possible that some rabbits might have returned, undisturbed by my previous stroll past their burrows.

I was right, but Sioux still showed no interest. Aimed at the solitary tree above the main concentration of ears poking up above the grass, instead he flapped yet again into the hedge. As I held up my fist for what seemed like the umpteenth time, I suddenly caught sight of a group of three rabbits eyeing me suspiciously. Two decided it was safer in the hedge, but – and here my heart leaped – the third bounced further away from the scrub. He disappeared behind a slight ridge, out of sight, but not mind. I was pretty sure there were no burrows beneath the scrap of bramble. It was the perfect opportunity for him. My pulse racing I cast Sioux forward – only for him to flap into the tangle of branches next to me. The rabbit thought better of his coverless position and scuttled into the hedge. Not for the first time I reached into my pocket, cursing. Pulling out a chick leg, I put it between my fingers and continued walking, not bothering to look back. He seemed more fired up now and I thought he would follow on with no problems. I scoured the field ahead for rabbits. Sure enough half a dozen were bouncing around the hedge a hundred yards further along.

Behind me Sioux gave his little squeak which indicates he is on his way. I waited for a second to see the pale flicker out of the corner of my eye and to feel his weight on my fist.

It didn't happen. Turning around, I saw him mantled on the ground, his wings wrapped forwards, pitching a feathered tent over the dusty, rabbit-scraped earth. He was screaming of course, but it had a different note than normal. It was now charged with pure adrenalin. Had I dropped a piece of meat? He looked as if he had caught something, but this was impossible. After all, only a second before I had walked over the same piece of ground. I would have trodden on anything crouching in the shortcropped turf.

But he had caught something – a rabbit! His foot was locked tightly around its head, his claws driven into the creature's neck and skull. He was triumphant and resentful, more worried that I might try to take it off him than by the still twitching form. Staring at me in fury, he hopped on one foot towards the hedge, dragging the grey bundle behind him in the other. It seemed tiny, barely two months old at a guess and probably on one of its first outings. In size it was barely bigger than the rat he had dispatched for me, probably weighing about four ounces. Not exactly impressive, but it was at any rate a kill.

This was not how I had imagined it. There was no powder snow and the flight had been less than spectacular – indeed

141

although it had taken place within five yards of me, I hadn't even seen it!

Nevertheless, it was a real kill, his first legitimate catch and done on his own initiative from start to finish. Picking him up gingerly with the corpse still gripped tightly in his bunched foot, I walked back to the car, jealous defiance screamed at me all the way. I put both bird and prey in the carrying box.

By the time we got back to the cottage he'd broken into the body, the edges of his mouth stained with blood, the rabbit's head and shoulders substantially reduced in volume. I allowed him to keep the head, but managed deftly to remove the rest of the corpse without his spotting the theft. With this under his belt, he should be keen as mustard tomorrow and there is no point in spoiling potential flights by allowing weight to mar his edge. And already there seems to be a new glint in his eye, a sharpness in the way he stares at the great tits that flit around the flower beds.

But best of all, as I threw the ball for the dogs within sight of him, my exertions were greeted by his total, deafening silence.

Thursday 18 March

MY SOLITUDE was broken by Mick and Phil who came around for dinner. They were late and apologetic, but the unspoken undercurrent was that it was my fault. Phil pointed out that the first he'd known of it was when I'd mentioned it to him on Monday. That was, I had to admit, true. I'd fixed the date originally with Mick on Sunday night after Phil had retired in a bad way, following a drinking bout with *The King's Head*'s landlord and wife that had lasted all day. Mick, it transpired, had since forgotten – or rather the news had never registered with him. He was too drunk that evening to have taken note of anything, having spent the day at Cheltenham races.

This evening I was surprised to find he was sober. He had no appetite, however, having already eaten in Woodstock. He was slightly shamefaced about forgetting, but nevertheless, he too seemed to think that it was my fault. 'Fancy 'spectin' me to remember tha' Daniel,' he laughed. 'You saw how I was on Sunday!' He had a point. He had been propped up on the bar by ten o'clock, eyelids drooping, but speech only slightly slurred. The dinner party was not a great triumph. The food was dried out because of the delay and Mick's earlier meal made it difficult for him to force down more than a few mouthfuls. A touch dismayed, I thought that at least an appearance by Sioux would liven things up and brought him in. He was looking particularly impressive. With his feathers fluffed up against the chill of the night air, the hawk looked twice his normal size. As might be expected he was screaming, but I was still proud and looked to the two men for signs of approval.

The effect was not quite what I had hoped for. Phil seemed fairly interested, but Mick just looked a little puzzled.

'Oi'm sorry Daniel, Oi just can't see the attraction,' he said sadly, shaking his head. 'Whoi don' you do something sensible, like football or cricket?'

Normally I would have sprung to the defence of falconry, but the combination of the failure of the meal and Sioux's triumphal entry had depressed me. I was like a proud parent whose child had just been criticised: crushed and low in spirits.

Monday 22 March

THE CONTINUING OBSESSION with the hawk is beginning to alarm even me. This afternoon I went into Oxford, in theory to feed my mother, but in practice to visit Blackwells. It was well worth the trip, with two of the host of falconry books I've been searching for on the shelves – and one was even half price. Naturally I bought both and, fired up with enthusiasm, sent off for four more. Although totally broke, I seem to have just spent well over £100 on six books devoted to hawks.

In the same vein, I used the excuse of spending time with my godson and namesake, Daniel, to go to a falconry centre at the weekend. His parents, my cousin Lawrence and his Japanese wife, have just returned to Oxford from Tokyo, together with their two children. Two more delightful boys would be difficult to imagine. They are constantly happy, their faces painted with perpetual broad smiles. Beautifully polite, dark-eyed and incredibly good-looking – they are altogether a delight to be with. Together with their father, we drove across the Cotswolds to the National Birds of Prey Centre.

It was my first visit since the kestrel left my life. I'd been once during the brief spell when she perched in the back garden, but after she flew off, I was at first too distraught to visit the place. And then as the pain of the bird's departure faded, so too did my memories of the Centre's attractions. I was also rarely in that corner of Gloucestershire, but the distant recollection of the place was resurrected by one of the falconry books from Blackwells which was written by its owner.

As so often happens when things are arranged well in advance, the weather was bad. This was a mixed blessing. On the one hand it threatened to impair, or possibly even prevent, the flying demonstration. But on the other it would keep the numbers of visitors down: and my loathing of crowds has only increased since my move out to the country-side. Most important of all, however, it meant that I was not losing any of my own flying-time. Neither Sioux nor rabbits like the damp.

I enjoyed the trip, in spite of the appalling weather. The day was punctuated by squalls of rain which peppered us as we drove across the high ground above Gloucester. Nevertheless, we still caught two flying displays and enjoyed the day thoroughly (at least I certainly did). In my dimly remembered trip as a ten year-old, I had slightly disliked the Centre's owner. I found her manner irritating, the jokes unfunny and predictable. But I now revised my opinion. It must be difficult to explain the basics of falconry to a crowd which contains a wide spread of knowledge, ranging from the total ignoramus to the falconer with twenty years' experience beneath his belt.

I am far from an expert, but at least I have read extensively on the subject and fly my own bird. Nevertheless I learnt a fair amount from both displays. One of the best parts, for example, was the display she described as the 'unimpressive' flying of a falcon in early training. Certainly it might be nothing compared to the saker/peregrine hybrid which flew first, but it was fascinating in its own right, particularly in view of my thoughts of a new falcon for the summer.

I was not alone in my impressions. Hugh, the elder child, decided he wanted either a computer or an eagle, and Daniel reckoned that nothing less than an Andean condor would satisfy him. It was wonderful seeing his eyes light up with wonder at the size of the latter. Although I went anxious to get some advice on dealing with Sioux, the opportunity to ask questions after the first flight was not the occasion (everyone else was crowding around the bird with queries such as: 'Can they see in the dark?' 'What do they eat normally?'). So Daniel and I wandered off towards the breeding pens. In the second was the condor – standing three feet high and with a huge eleven foot wingspan. He was a full sexual imprint (reared so close to humans that he now believed mankind and condors to be the same thing). He was full of the joys of spring – and he took a particular shine to the seven-year-old Daniel.

The boy was, after all, about the same size as him (minus the wings of course). To the consternation of the latter, he came swooping down to the front of the pen, his wing beats whipping up the sawdust in little whirlwinds on the floor of the pen and ruffling the child's hair. Daniel squeaked in surprise and claimed he was frightened, yet returned time and again to the pen for the rest of the visit, each time giving delighted little shrieks as the randy bird flapped towards him.

The demonstrations were definitely the highlight, however, and at the end of the final show, I rushed up to Jemima, the owner, as she stalked off to the entrance. Her manner was abrupt, but this is her natural way. The replies became more courteous as she reached the main building. There were three or four questions I was desperate to have answered: What was the range of male red tail weights (i.e. was Sioux big or little for his species)? She didn't know: 'Couldn't tell you – haven't flown enough,' she barked. Should I moult him out in an aviary or could I fly him through the moult as her father suggested in his book? Perhaps she misunderstood me: 'If you don't moult him he'll look very ragged by the end of the year,' she snapped. 'Do you have an aviary? Well, put him in that and moult him out in there.' By now we were back by the shop and she'd relaxed somewhat. 'Frank over there flies a female red tail.' She nodded at a young assistant seated on a bench with a child he was obviously teaching about falconry, a lanner perched on his fist. 'They're very quick,' smiled Frank. 'Personally I reckon they're underrated and quicker than a Harris.' (Harris hawks are now the most popular hunting bird in Britain – manoeuvrable, big enough to take most of the available quarry species and extremely good-tempered.)

Finally I asked if she had any suggestions about stopping the dreadful screaming. I explained I wasn't sure if he was an imprint, or whether he'd simply begun screaming out of frustration and boredom. 'Is he aggressive?' she asked.

I was not sure. Certainly he mantled more than her birds, covering up any food with his wings, shielding it from perceived attempts to steal it. He had also, after all, footed me horribly before Christmas. And he had been very 'sticky-footed' during his training. So undoubtedly he was more aggressive than her birds, but did this constitute aggression? He was a hawk after all. Was his behaviour normal and hers just very well behaved? It all depended on what you measure him against. I shrugged my shoulders trying to disguise my confusion and obvious ignorance. 'A bit,' I said.

'Try feeding him up and moulting him quickly,' she suggested. 'Our Harrises are entirely parent-reared but are still prone to scream if their weight is brought down too gradually. If you keep them hungry but inactive for too long it can make them start screaming out of frustration. The same would be true for red tails – it's possible to get them vocal after three or even four years if you muck them around for too long.'

Now I am told. Why the hell has no one warned me about

the possibility of late-imprinting? There is nothing about it in any of the books. Only the out-dated White gave any real feel of the endless difficulties of training a hawk, but of course I had ignored his trials, believing myself better-equipped. In retrospect I should have taken the hint and been less arrogant.

I pondered all this on the drive home, returning far too late to make the evening flight. Indeed I was so late that I only just made the pub by closing time. It was a frosty night and as a result the toads were not littering the road as they have been recently. Nevertheless, I was travelling very slowly as I turned up the hill at the bottom of the lane. Caught in the headlights was the bouncing rear of a creature, a dull mousey grey in tone. At first I thought it was a fox, but it was too short and fat and its gait too bumpy. A cat? No, not unless it was a Manx, for I caught sight of a stumpy little tail. Surely it couldn't be . . .?

And then it turned, presenting a clear side view, the sharp snout half turned towards me. The unmistakable profile and black and white of a badger – my first ever sighting and within a couple of hundred yards of the cottage! It turned into the gardens of the former farm buildings to continue its search for worms and frogs. It was a good end to a good day.

Part Three

MOULTING

Wednesday 7 April

IT WAS WITH very mixed feelings that I put Sioux in to moult this morning. The decision was prompted by the advice of every hawk expert I have spoken to over the last few weeks. All the literary evidence pushes in the same direction. In common with most birds, red tails shed their feathers once a year, the avian equivalent of a service, replacing the tatty plumage with new, undamaged growth. In the wild this would have already happened, triggered by lengthening days and increased food intake as the hardships of winter are replaced by the plenty of spring. Sioux has yet to start moulting, however, and it is for me to bump-start the process. My reluctance so far has been caused by the knowledge that bumping up his weight means the end of our hunts.

There are four good reasons for this. Most important, he will need as much food as he can eat – and top quality fodder too. Stuffed like this, my glove will hold no appeal and flights will be impossible. Second, while his new feathers grow, they are delicate and easily damaged. A big tussle with a healthy buck could cause a year of problems. Third, as the grass grows long and the trees sprout lush foliage, finding quarry will be difficult and losing the hawk easy. It would also make watching the flights difficult. Finally there has been a marked reduction in the number of rabbits at my best hunting site. In part this must be due to Chris and Stuart making an effort to cut their numbers down before the height of the breeding season, but the main reason is that they are getting wise to our approach. Either that or, as dawn gets earlier and earlier, Sioux and I are just not getting there in good enough time. In any event flights are becoming scarce and I think I might as well give the rabbits a chance to pick up in numbers.

So now is the time to stop hunting him and instead feed him as much as possible. In theory this will speed up the moult. The quicker he casts his feathers, the quicker he can fly again. This is a particularly important factor in view of the invitation I have received to spend two weeks in September on an estate in the Hebrides. With luck it will be awash with rabbits: most of the Western Isles are over-run with the creatures and I am desperate for him to be at full flying ability by then.

Nevertheless, it was with a heavy heart that I took the plunge, the only real attraction being Jemima's advice. Moulting him out properly and then bringing him back down to weight sharply just might, she thought, shut him up. In theory this runs counter to all the information on imprinting I have ever read. Once a screamer always a screamer is the general consensus and the advice is to avoid them like the plague. But I have just found a backer for her idea. The package of books that I ordered a few days ago has arrived, among them a collection of essays by American falconers. In this, the red tail specialist warns that they are so bright and easily tamed that they can become semi-imprinted very late as they realise that their owner provides food and company just as their parents did.

The thought that he might stop screaming is so attractive that after brooding on the moult for the past few days, I put him in his pen along with four chicks. It was not until the idea was suggested to me that I realised the full extent of how much I hate that scream. I have become fairly inured to it, but I can't pretend to like it in the slightest. Not only does it penetrate the innermost recesses of even my adjusted skull (and severely affects others who come along to watch), but it warns the rabbits and, most importantly of all, spoils a large part of the enjoyment of hunting – being finely tuned to the joys of nature.

The whole issue of his noise has given me a further insight into the sport. As I pored over the book, drinking in the descriptions of the red tail, I realised how little the British experts understand foreign birds. I should have twigged earlier to the possibility, I suppose, but like White before me, was always too ready to follow slavishly the advice of the experts. The fact is that most of them have limited experience of flying the lowly buzzards. After all, red tails have only been widely available in this country for a fairly short space of time and most British falconers had long-since learnt their craft by the time they arrived.

Things may have moved on since Abbess Juliana's description of a 'falconry pecking order', but with good reason some birds are more highly regarded than others. If you know what you are doing, there are much more appealing subjects than a buzzard – even a 'super-charged' version, as one expert describes the red tail. Today this would probably be a gos or Harris hawk. The latter is a form of buzzard, it is true, but unique in the world of falconry, it is highly sociable, naturally operating in family groups, and therefore well-suited to hunting with humans and even other Harrises. In addition it has an easy going temperament and a quarry-range that is ideal for the English hunting scene.

The goshawk has always been highly rated, fiery and fast, and there can be no question but that it is one of the most attractive raptors. Furthermore, as White would testify, it is wilder and a greater challenge to train. If this is intimidating to the beginner, it is an attraction to the experienced falconer. As a result, I suspect that none of the top British authorities has much experience of flying (as opposed to keeping) red tails.

More importantly, no one says that if you take a bird's weight down too slowly they can begin to scream, particularly red tails. In fact the reverse is true: they warn you not to drop them too fast, imaginations no doubt aflame with images of the skeletal corpses of birds whose owners have crassly starved them to death. Although conversations with Jack back the idea that slow weight loss can produce undesirable side effects, the threat is omitted from the printed advice. Add to this the American warning that a red tail is the most individualistic of all birds of prey, with no two birds having the same temperament, and one has a situation where the advice of British experts may be a little suspect – at least in its fine detail.

There might be a lot of idiotic owners out there, but I think that it would take a particularly silly falconer to kill his prize and joy through malnourishment. No, I fell into the trap of trying to fly him at as high a weight as possible. Unlike White, I was alert to the dangers of over-feeding and aware of the need to weigh him daily. But, like the author in whose footsteps I followed, I was too delighted to see him feed off my fist, too pleased when he came to my call, too happy when he flew down from the tree. The slightest progress gave me too much pleasure to allow me to cut him down as quickly as I should. As a result throughout the winter he was constantly hungry while never quite keen enough to progress fast. I thought it better to go slowly and carefully: in reality all I was doing was allowing him to become dependent on me.

If my suspicions are correct, gradually he began to see me as the sole source of food and company. Although this is exactly what the books tell you to aim for, in this case I had pushed him into increasingly vocal displays towards me, his food provider and companion. In my caution, I had unwittingly imprinted him, made him as hooked and unreliable as a heroin addict. It was for me to provide the detoxification.

Yet this is all wisdom after the event. I am the owner of a noisy, bad-tempered hawk, trying to rectify the situation by moulting him as advised. This means that I am now deprived of Sioux's flight for at least two or three months, possibly more, reduced to passive contemplation of my fat, silent hawk, and brooding on the lack of warning.

Monday 13 April

IT WAS AS I drove up the lane this morning, returning from a shopping trip, that I disturbed a partridge from the neighbour's garden. It tumbled down into the lane and scampered along in front of the car before bursting into flight, its stumpy body, so comical and ungainly on the ground – almost puffin-like – transformed in flight.

It was one of the pair that have established a territory in the field above the cottage and can often be seen scurrying along the road above the village, disturbed as they scrape at the grit on the road. They are red-legged partridges, 'Frenchies' as Chris calls them, their grey, common or 'English', cousins being rare around here.

For a moment I couldn't see its partner and was worried for it, but then caught a glimpse of it to the side of the car as it too powered away, but in the opposite direction. An hour later, as I sit at the word processor, I am watching the two creatures in the field before me, heads peering towards each other over the tops of the grass, separated by a couple of hundred yards. One can almost feel their anxiety to be reunited.

It is at moments like this that it is all too easy to be anthropomorphic: these two small, fat birds, their faces painted like marionettes, eye-lined and sideburned, rushing towards each other, wings held forwards like arms, crying with joy and relief as they draw closer. It is so tempting to dub in the '*Jacques! Jacques! Tu vives!*' and the reply '*Fifi – c'est pas possible! . . . Mais tu m'aime encore?*'

Tempting though this may be, it would of course be a mistake. They are driven by the simple desire to reproduce. Having spent a great deal of time and effort over the past few months selecting each other and establishing a territory, they can't afford the loss of the investment. With, who knows, a nest of anything up to twenty eggs close by, the death of a partner means not only the end of the clutch (it would be almost impossible for one bird to rear the chicks alone) but, more important, it would represent a wasted year – breeding-wise at any rate.

So as Jacques and Fifi scamper together, their cries are not of love but rather of selfish satisfaction and relief. Delight that all has not been in vain and that the genes may yet survive.

Saturday 24 April

IT MAY BE my imagination, but I am beginning to suspect that being unable to fly the bird is undermining my health and work. Now I find myself languishing in bed, lying there until eight or nine. This seems appallingly lazy and I can't help comparing my low productivity with the gloriously heavy output during the two weeks after my return from Beirut. Instead of getting up at dawn, flying Sioux, buying a paper, making a cup of tea and sitting down at the computer by eight, I am now lounging around the house doing the chores until almost midday, before eventually turning to money-earning matters.

And when working, I make cups of tea far more frequently than I would normally, with kettle-boiling providing natural punctuation points to my day. As I wait for it to heat, the delay is a natural time to check up on the progress of Sioux's moult. Although I have been trying to break the way he associates me with food for the sake of shutting him up, I still visit him five or six times a day, ostensibly to check up on his plumage, but in reality merely to feast my eyes.

About a week ago while I was performing this ritual visit, I was disturbed from my reverie by Havoc barking her heart out in the field behind the pen. Imagining yet again that the cattle were the cause of her excitement and that she was driving them up the field, I shot out of the hawk's pen to check, cursing her as I stumbled across the stile.

It was worse – the farmer was inspecting his herd and it was he, not the cattle, who was the object of her fury as she sprang around, stiff-legged in front of him. Grizzled and wrapped in an old raincoat fastened around the waist with string, he was staring balefully at her. Fortunately she came back quickly and I shunted her inside before rushing back outside to apologise.

He stared at me suspiciously as I strode purposefully across the field, but loosened as I talked. I apologised, explaining that she was still a puppy and it had been he, rather than the cattle, that she was barking at. I had just about managed to break her to stock, I explained, but she was at heart a guard dog and was alerting me. He nodded, but said the cattle were about to calf, the request to make sure she didn't bother them implicit in his words, which were almost a parody of a rustic character – short-sentenced, repetitive and delivered in an accent so thick I found it difficult to follow him.

As I turned to go, I asked politely what breed of cattle they were.

'Long'orns and long'orn crarsses,' he said tersely, but without any hint of animosity. 'Tham's the crarsses.' He pointed to three swollen cows, moth-eaten with ringworm, munching a few yards away.

I have begun to dream seriously of selling my flat and moving out to the countryside full-time. Vague thoughts of livestock were filling my dreaming moments and I was particularly curious about rare breeds. Why, I asked, did he keep them? Were they valuable in their own right, or did they command a premium at Smithfield?

'Oi woun' know about tha',' he said. 'Thy'se 'ardy thoo, very 'ardy. Thiz bin ow arl win'er – thy ain' bin insoide.'

With the conversation flagging somewhat, I apologised once again to him for Havoc's behaviour, but by now he'd decided he liked me. It would be misleading to say that he was in full flow, more on a roll – like a tractor parked on a lightly-sloping hill with the handbrake off.

"Thy'se hardy – dun woorry 'bou' dawg. Now yo knows oi wun' shoon 'un,' he said, lumbering on. 'Bu' dawgs cun be prawblem. Shaw two thiz win'er. Up Chippy aer'drum. Traveller dawgs.' He paused for a moment to spit with feeling. 'Barstards!!! New age – thy dun care 'bou' no animarls. Thy kill two me sheep and bi' cows' ankles till thyse raw. Cou'n work ow whoi 'ey wou'n come ow' bushes fur week.'

I was clearly showing my alarm, because he paused and again promised not to shoot Havoc should he see her worrying his cattle, but he continued to mutter about the travellers. The gun always went with him when he inspected any of his stock near their latest encampment, he said. From his tone it was clear that this was not a precautionary measure, but rather in the hope that a shot might present itself.

Later investigations reveal that he is notorious for this. He owns the land on which the local tip is found and I'd thought vaguely of asking him for permission to hunt on his land, but had been warned that he forms opinions of strangers within the first couple of minutes which he then holds with a fierce tenacity. His dislike of the travellers is, it transpires, more of the nature of a family feud than a shepherd's protective urges towards his flock.

His son apparently caught some of them totting on the tip. There was an argument and fists flew. The local man got the worst of it, but was not prepared to forget. He returned with his gun and blasted their van at short range, firing into the radiator to frighten the entire bunch before turning the gun on one of them who was skulking, terrified, behind the bus. He waited until the man had scampered to the relatively safety of sixty or so yards and then let loose, peppering his backside with number six shot.

Both incidents are deeply etched in his father's memory: although he probably objects most to the subsequent loss of his son's shotgun licence. The fact that this and a hundred pound fine are the only punishment for shooting someone only indicates the level of antipathy towards the travellers at all levels.

I can't share his hatred. Like the swallows and martins that are beginning to nest under the eaves of the houses in the town, travellers are a sign of the season. For the last ten years or so, they have reappeared in the locality each summer, wandering the countryside in a makeshift collection of vans and lorries. They live off the land to a certain extent, dabbling at the edges of the scrap trade, maybe begging a little and certainly claiming benefits. None of this goes down well with the deeply conservative locals. They have little or no conception of urban homelessness, poverty and deprivation.

To them, the 'new agers' are merely dirty semi-criminals, parasites who refuse to do an honest day's work and who have deliberately left the conventional family home to lead a self-indulgent wandering life.

The rebel in me likes travellers for succeeding where the Opposition has failed. They have disturbed the complacency of prosperous Britain; a reminder of its embarrassing failures with the poor, they have threatened it in the most peaceful of ways. And I admire them for their freedom, the wandering life. Bruce Chatwin is right in *Songlines* when he talks of man as a nomad. There, buried in all of us is the roaming spirit. Maybe this is one element of man's long-standing fascination with hawks – he is jealous of their lack of chains, their freedom to wander. Surely it is no coincidence that some of the most revered raptors are the big, far-ranging falcons – the gyrs, sakers and peregrines? After all the name of the last, the most prestigious hunting-bird in European falconry, means wanderer. Outside the breeding season they can roam over huge distances, seemingly at random, unlike a migratory bird or one merely in search of a new hunting territory.

Saturday 26 April

WHEN I FIRST put Sioux in the pen, I went to extraordinary lengths to break his associations of me and food. I hid rats under scraps of paper with string tied around their torsos. Then, when out of sight, I would pull the unfortunate corpse in one last indignity across the floor of the pen. Fired by the movement, Sioux would pounce on the body, driving his talons clear through it as he needlessly crushed out its life. Just as with his rabbit, he then mantled over his prey, wings umbrellaed, screaming out his resentment, while I, crouched outside the pen, watched quietly.

This morning, as I was congratulating myself for this ingenious way of boosting his confidence, I heard a sound behind me. It was Muffin running around in his pen, standing up at the wire now and again, claws curling through the mesh. To my left, through the glass Sioux was crouched over his latest rat, his feathers fluffed up as he imagined its death throes. I suddenly realised what I was doing. These are creatures bred for the clean world of the laboratory: albinos, as white and pink-eyed as the ferret.

Given that the whole reason for the pale ferret is so that the hawk doesn't mistake hunter for hunted, feeding white rats may well prove a serious mistake next season. Let's hope that by then Sioux has forgotten the lesson. Perhaps I should colour them brown in future? No, maybe not. Even I flinch at the idea of dipping deep-frozen cadavers into a vat of brown food dye.

In the meantime, there is no point in continuing with the grisly charade of pulling cadavers across the floor of his pen. To begin with, he is no longer hungry enough to pounce on the food immediately, but instead stares at it with disdain when I put it on the log that serves as his table. Long after I have disappeared back into the house, reluctantly returning to the latest article on some subject in which I have little knowledge and still less interest, he descends to inspect the offering. If it meets with his approval, he grasps it in his massive feet, flying up to a favourite perch on Dad's bicycle handle to pluck it. He seems to prefer the rats and quails to chicks, perhaps bored by the non-stop diet of yellow-fluff between Christmas and Easter. Whatever he's eating, he always begins with the head, pulling the feathers or fur off in delicate little tufts. In consequence the floor is littered with tiny feathers and white hairs, while the bicycle spokes are streaked with the yolk that lies underneath each chick's chest.

When I put him into the pen, somehow I had hoped that he would begin to moult within a few days, but instead it took two weeks before the first secondaries dropped. Although I followed the books' advice slavishly, feeding him with as much high-quality food as I could and leaving him in a moulting enclosure big enough to allow him to flap around at will, his metabolism remained stubbornly sluggish. I made further enquiries of anyone I thought might be knowledgeable on the subject, but received little encouragement. At the falconry centre they said he should be finished in about three months

– or at the end of June. To me this seemed like an eternity, one that could only be borne because it was unavoidable, nature's equivalent of an annual service and MOT.

Telephone calls to Jack and chats with a couple of other local falconers reveal that this is probably optimistic in the extreme. Every bird moults differently, they said, and you've just got to allow yours to do it in his own fashion. Certainly you can help with good-quality food; a big pen to allow him to exercise, getting the blood to the outermost tips of his wings; and plenty of light, but beyond this there is nothing that the falconer can do. A friend of Jack's said that his goshawk would only begin moulting in July, regardless of feeding, but then pushed out all its new feathers in a matter of five weeks and was ready to fly by the end of August. It has done this for the past fifteen years without exception and nothing has ever made any difference.

'Don't worry, yours'll be finished by September,' he cooed reassuringly to me.

September! Five months away. Each of his best flights during the winter flashed in front of my eyes and I felt almost physically sick at the thought. Five long months without being able to fly him at all ! A whole spring and summer with none of the pleasure of seeing him row his way across fields, fold his wings and plummet to the fist from the tree tops! An eternity, a lifetime before I can see him rocketing after a disappearing scut. I quickly phoned up another two falconers I'd heard of. I was like a patient who's been told the condition is terminal. I was desperate for a second, more favourable, opinion. But his advice was only echoed by the others, all of whom guessed that it would be four to five months before I could fly him.

I am pleased to say, however, that subsequent events seem to have proved this vision unduly pessimistic. After his worrying period of inaction, Sioux's moult has begun and is progressing apace. Most raptors have about fifty crucial flight feathers, twelve in the tail, with twenty or so on each wing. The important ones are those on the trailing edge of the wing and these are divided into *secondaries* which are those closest to the body and the *primaries* which are the outer ones. The former are of more uniform length and have rounded tips, the latter more pointed and varied in length both between each other and, more particularly, between species. Obviously the bird has to lose its feathers one by one: if they were all to be shed at once not only would the hawk be bald (and very chilly), but incapable of flight and therefore of catching its food. The sequence is also staggered, of course, normally beginning with the secondaries, then moving on to the primaries with the tail (or more properly *deck* feathers) beginning about halfway through the replacement of the primaries. As each new feather reaches about a third of its eventual length the next replaces it and so on. As a result the bird is never missing more than a few feathers, with perhaps the same number of partially-grown neighbours.

Until Sioux began to moult I'd never taken any notice of how ragged most birds become in the spring and early summer, but now I am much more aware of it. Looking out of the window I see most of the local birds are looking distinctly patchy. In particular the jackdaws nesting nearby and, on my rare trips into London, the huge carrion crows that soar over Hyde Park, seem scrappy. But as the months progress, one sees, with a definite sense of excitement, that gap in the feathers move along the wing. At present it is two-thirds of the way towards the tip. Seeing this for the first time, I feel almost as if I've been let into a great secret. It is as if, through my relationship with Sioux, I've been granted membership of some exclusive club, introduced to the wisdom of generations of falconers from across the world. I feel like a privileged pupil.

Tuesday 28 April

SUBSEQUENT TO LAST week's conversation with the farmer and my ponderings on travellers, I paid more than passing attention to the three horsedrawn caravans pulled up outside Woodstock on Sunday. They were parked on a wide verge, ponies quietly cropping the lush grass that would otherwise go to waste. There on the side of one of the pretty cylindrical tops was a crude sign – 'Lurcher Pups for Sale'.

Bel and I were on our way to drop off a friend at Oxford station and by the time I returned, an hour later, I had made up my mind. Pulling over I walked across to inspect the pups which were corralled into a pen of chicken wire. The travellers were clean, polite and friendly, the antithesis of the local farmer's objections. They had made their own caravans, lived with a handful of dogs and chickens and were waiting for Stow fair to begin. I liked their spokesman, who talked in a quiet but confident tone.

'£30, take it or leave it,' were his first words. I nodded and inspected the litter of seven-week-old puppies.

I had wanted a bitch, but the two left were pied – white patched with rust – and both were short-coated. The dogs were much more pleasantly coloured, one black and tan, the other foxy. I instantly fell in love with the latter. The price was reasonable enough, but as a matter of principle I objected.

'£30 seems a bit high,' I lied, betraying my reluctance to haggle with the offer. 'What would you say to £25?'

'Done.' He too had no energy.

So I now have three dogs, a hawk and a ferret. Mind you, judging from Sioux's looks at the puppy this morning as I paid my usual trip of homage to him, tiny dog trotting at heel, unless I am careful to keep the two separated for the next couple of weeks, I will soon be back to a pair. The sight of the lurcher prompted a rare burst of energy from the bird and he actually flew to the perch nearest the door, teetering on the very edge, leaning forward, eyes focused sharply on the small, rabbit-sized, brown form next to the door, his body tensed.

I bundled the puppy away quickly. Although the door was closed and therefore he was in no danger, I don't want Sioux damaging himself in a headlong fling. Additionally, for all my pride in being close to the balance of nature, to life and death, there is something more than a little disquieting in the thought that the hawk wants to kill and eat another valued member of my menagerie. I mean, I could cope with a hen or duck disappearing down one of my predators, but for one to fall prey to another feels rather different.

On the encouraging side, however, his moult is now in full swing and the floor is littered with the signs. Although it is only a matter of a few days since the first large feather was thrown, so many have followed that he seems to be rocketing along. Of course I have no experience and therefore no yard-stick against which to measure his progress, but I think he might even be on his primaries by now. It is infuriatingly difficult to work out however. To try to confirm matters, I have been entering the pen, prodding him into flight, trying to glimpse the gaps in his wings as he flaps across the room with two quick wingbeats. There seems to be a break about halfway along his wings. If this is the case, he is moulting very fast and might even be halfway through.

Maybe he will make rapid – no record-breaking – pro-gress, and will be finished in three months? In fact, if I am right and he is shedding primaries only a couple of weeks or so after he dropped his first secondary, he might be finished by the end of May, not June!

But I am day-dreaming again. There are an awful lot of 'ifs' in my speculation. Trying to keep my bounding hopes under control, I keep having to remind myself that this means he could be flying again after only two months: far too good to be true. Most experts say five months is a fair timespan for a hawk's moult. With luck, however, he'll be hunting again in July.

The prospect is the more appealing because last week I rode my bicycle into town. Feeling sorry for the dogs, I got them to run alongside and in consequence took the bridlepath past the field where Sioux caught the rabbit. The holes were on the other side of the valley, a good couple of hundred yards away. It was five on a Friday afternoon, broad daylight on a sunny spring day and not a good time to spot rabbits. But there, out in the open, twenty yards from their holes, were five or six fully-grown bunnies, with a speckling of tiny brown flecks around them which looked suspiciously like this year's kits. Obviously Chris was right when he said that although he'd been hitting them hard, there had been rabbits in that hedge for a hundred years and whatever he did they would be there in a century's time.

It is of course a reminder of the creature's incredible reproductive capabilities. Townsfolk tend to say glibly that so-and-so breeds like a rabbit, but most are ignorant of the full scale of what this means. They can breed at three months old, producing litters of anything up to eight. As soon as the doe has given birth she comes into season again. Although reproduction is affected by the seasons, in mild winters, places where food is abundant or the warren particularly warm and dry, they can reproduce all year round. With a lifespan of say, three years, it has been calculated that one pair of rabbits could become one million in three years under ideal conditions (or three million if you take another's figures). That of course is a theoretical reproduction rate. Field studies in New Zealand suggest that a healthy doe rarely manages more than twenty-five youngsters a year . . . all the same, twenty-five!

By July these local kits will be almost fully-grown and the does among them will have litters of their own. It might sound callous, but Sioux will find the smaller and more inexperienced rabbits easy to catch and this will get him into form for the winter. Perhaps I am day-dreaming again, but for some reason I feel certain that next year is going to be very different from our first and that we are going to have a good measure of success. In the meanwhile, looking at him in the shed staring at the puppy, there can be no worries that he has lost the desire to hunt.

The little dog, meanwhile, seems to be growing almost day by day, with his future lurcher shape still disguised but recognisable under his almost feline form. After some thought, I've called him Bracken.

Saturday 1 May

HOWEVER MUCH I may have transferred my attentions to the puppy, there can be no denying that I am still hypnotised by Sioux as he sits out there in the shed, dropping feathers.

My mood of wild optimism about being able to fly him by the end of the month has swung around to pessimism now, mainly because the flurry of feathers which started his moult (anything up to four a day being dropped) has dried up over the last couple of days.

He is silent now of course – or at least his screams have ceased, to be replaced with a strange little chirping sound, more suited to a budgerigar than a buzzard. This is only to be expected, given that he now has more good quality food than he can eat. Now I am greeted with a series of little chortles and gurgles when I enter the pen, tilting his head to one side and the other, eyeing my hands eagerly for the latest morsel that I might have for him.

All this, of course, is scant consolation. Instead I am reduced to waiting impatiently for the end of the moult and cursing my enforced inactivity. When I began his training last October I had no idea how absorbed I would become, nor how rapidly it would take over my life. Instead, if anything I was worried that he would be a temporary plaything, something that I would become bored with. Now, however, I know there is nothing for it. I know I'm going to have to go ahead with my falcon plan. I think there are a few fields locally that are just large enough to be able to fly crows, although the bird might find it a bit on the tight side.

When we talked last, Jack told me to get a falcon as a bird which would complement Sioux, rather than distract from the never-ending training process. In addition, I would be aiming for different quarry – birds such as crows and seagulls – and so there would be no competition for quarry. By that I mean if one were to have two rabbit-hunting hawks, and managed to fly both of them at their best without favouring one or the other, each time one caught a rabbit, it would be one less for the other. But if I get a falcon, I will be flying it at birds that no red tail has a hope of catching.

The thought is so, so tempting.

Monday 3 May

SINCE THE BEGINNING of April I have found myself reading and re-reading every word I have on falconry and falcons. I have also been making trips to Newent on the slightest excuse. Over the past couple of weeks I have been there three times, each as good as the last.

Of particular interest on my last visit was the explanation about the search for thermals. These are the columns of hot air rising from the land, warmed by the sun in vast convection currents. By opening its wings and circling in the column of heat, the bird can rise to incredible heights with little or no expenditure of energy. From thousands of feet up it commands a huge area in every respect. Not only can it see far more potential prey, but with the advantage of height it is able to plummet down on creatures with which, in level pursuit, it would be equally matched.

While the broadwings, such as eagles, buzzards and vultures are the great practitioners of this, almost all diurnal raptors use them. Unfortunately on every visit so far the weather has been chilly and overcast, with thermals rare in consequence, but last time I was there a saker/peregrine hybrid put on a good display of finding one. Normally a falcon flies with fast wing beats, working hard to pick up hunting speed. But on this occasion the bird flew into a thermal. Suddenly his fluttering wings froze as if paralysed, stretched to their limits as they caught the warm air. He rose sharply as if pulled heavenwards by an invisible deity. Banking, he circled, seemingly ever upwards, but the climb was brought to a halt by the weak current running out at about a thousand feet.

Having been alerted to this trait, I have just spent the morning watching the local kestrel in a new light. He was fluttering over the field next to the cottage, before suddenly tumbling on some tiny creature. When he rose from the grass that had obscured him, I followed his flight carefully, wondering whether he had a partner and if so, where they were nesting. But instead of flying off with his prey clenched in his feet, his flight showed the dive had been unsuccessful.

He fluttered upwards, working hard to gain altitude, but instead of checking to hover, his wings suddenly stiffened and he began to rise sharply in the weak May sunshine. Up he went – and up, climbing steadily, above the tree tops and beyond. Normally a kestrel hunts below a hundred feet or so, hovering for a while over one patch of ground before moving to the next. There is little incentive to get too high – its prey is rarely in the open for more than a few seconds and however fast it tumbles out of the sky, if too far up it will miss its opportunity. But this bird was clearly enjoying himself too much. With his wings outstretched he described huge circles in the hazy air, rising rapidly until little more than a speck, far too high to have a hope of hunting, but nevertheless revelling in such effortless flight.

Watching him, I was reminded of another of the warnings about red tails – they frequently get carried away if they hit a thermal. However sharp set and eager to hunt, in such conditions they can forget about pursuit, drawn instead into a sort of soaring reverie, rising higher and higher, blind and deaf to the falconer's entreaties. This is highly undesirable and frustrating, remark the experts sternly.

I could not agree. However keen to hunt, however many rabbits might be around, I would love to see him soaring, rising to a height where his four-foot wingspan became a dot in the sky. I could sit for hours watching him floating there and it is yet another reason why I long for him to finish the moult before the end of the summer thermals. I fly him for the beauty of his flight, for the sheer majesty of his movement, be it chasing a rabbit or coasting down on to the fist on motionless wings. To add soaring to the list would be wonderful.

Tuesday 4 May

A VISIT BY a party of my parents' friends proved a warning lesson – and I vowed to make a note not to get too carried away with the appeal of falconry. While most people are genuinely interested in Sioux when they first see him, asking intelligent questions about his training, I have yet to meet one who has the same reaction as I do. From almost the earliest moment I can remember, the sight of a hawk, even a kestrel, kindled my passions, firing me with a desperate desire to own and possess one myself.

None of the troop of admirers who have inspected Sioux since last October has asked excitedly how they can acquire one, what equipment they would need to purchase and who might help. And if no one has been inspired to take up the noble art themselves, several are positively turned off by the subject – particularly if exposed too frequently to the hawk. Indeed it is no exaggeration to say that I have probably lost friends, thanks to him. Hard as I try not to talk too much about it, whenever I am in a group – say a dinner party – falconry inevitably comes up. All it takes is for someone who doesn't know me or the bird to ask a question and I can't resist. All queries, however routine, seem to lead back to the hawk, even 'What do you do?'

This now produces the glib response: 'I'm a falconer who dabbles in journalism.' It is meant as a joke of course, something guaranteed to excite a reaction. I have years to go before I reach a level of expertise where I can genuinely describe myself as a falconer. Unfortunately it does reflect my priorities, however.

The more I talk, the more fired up I get. As I speak I can feel the exhilaration mounting. Describing a flight at a rabbit, the essentials of training or the ethics of hunting, my spirits begin to soar and I become almost drugged by my own words. In some ways it is like knocking back glasses of wine, with inhibitions evaporating. Normal rules of polite behaviour disappear. Gone are the guidelines which tell you to ask the stranger about themselves – what they do, what interests them and what their views on a range of subjects might be. Instead I am swept along by my own words, carried off by my descriptions into a sort of reverie where I trip over my own tongue in an attempt to paint as full a picture as possible.

Just as when getting drunk, I am aware that the process

is taking place, but feel almost distanced from it: an observer, watching disinterestedly from the sidelines. It's like seeing a favourite film for the fifth or sixth time – initially you don't feel involved, but are still unable to turn the television off. Gradually the plot takes hold.

I don't claim to be the world's most sensitive conversationalist, but at least I used to make an effort to interest other people – and tried to engage in some sort of dialogue. But mention the hawk and what might start as a conversation becomes a series of well-rehearsed answers to the inevitable queries. At first the answers are brief, but after a while they lengthen and I even find myself posing the most interesting questions on the other's behalf – after all, I know the best ones to ask.

As I contemplate my failings, I comfort myself that at least this is normally not too bad for my new acquaintance. Falconry is, after all, a fairly unusual subject and almost certainly the other person will be curious – at first. Even if I drone on for an hour, the quirkiness of the subject seems a reasonable compensation for the boredom of having to listen patiently, barely able to get a word in edgeways.

No, the people for whom I feel sorriest are my nearest and dearest. Friends and relatives in particular are subjected to the same patter over and over again. They have heard it all before many times and, like the Monty Python dead parrot sketch, most could fill in for me, acting as understudy to my obsessive.

In particular, Bel is almost angelic in her patience. Not only does she have to hear everything time and time again, but as the moult progresses she has been dragged along to Newent three times in six weeks: each trip three and a half hours in the car, plus at least two in the centre itself. To make matters worse, both her mother and stepfather are intrigued by the hawk, and thus whenever there is a social occasion, such as her sister's wedding or her own birthday, she is subjected to overhearing me engaged in earnest conversation on some aspect of falconry with one of her relatives. It must be bad enough to be buried in this obsession when on my 'territory', but almost unbearable when the sport follows her to London, to her own flat and family.

Instead she teases me gently about my failings, but lets me get on with it. Her forbearance is exceptional. My great aunt issued me with strictures not to mention either hawk or ferret again in my letters: 'because they frighten me', and another friend told me bluntly he doesn't want to have anything to do with me if the subject is going to crop up at all, let alone dominate the conversation. This effectively rules him out of my acquaintance of course. And I can't help noticing that Sioux is not a subject for the local pub, where the very mention is enough for the eyes of Mick and Phil to glaze over.

The more I think about it, the more the similarity with alcohol strikes me. Just as drink bowls you over with your own wit and repartee, so I get carried away when talking about the sport. And just as after a pub binge I might feel guilty about my behaviour, so I find myself cringing the next day when I try to remember anything at all about the person to whom I talked for so long.

Wednesday 5 May

I STILL PAY daily trips of homage to the hawk's pen, absorbing every detail. I've noted with fascination, for example, that when he eats a rat, he always starts with the head and shoulders, progressing to the vital organs and leaving the hindquarters to last. If anything, he seems to find the brain the choicest part, breaking into that first. In my enforced idleness everything I've read, each detail I observe, it all seems to gel together. Take this habit of eating the head. The books say that the falconer trying to train his goshawk to take hares should feed her rabbit and hare heads. This, they explain, will teach her to attack those parts of the creature that are least likely to be dislodged.

If Sioux's behaviour is anything to go by, this advice is superfluous. Hawks instinctively go for the head, be it alive or dead. Certainly on the occasion that Sioux attacked Dill during a training flight last December, it was her muzzle and shoulders that he gripped. For an instant he rode the surprised dog, hanging on side-saddle as she bolted across the field. She was in no danger of course (being the size of a small labrador), and he was shaken off quickly, but nevertheless it was the perfect grip to tackle big quarry.

It is an idle thought, but recalling the incident I can't help wondering about flying him at a hare next season. It might be possible: certainly female red tails can take on these big creatures and he is largish for a male. The idea has only been fuelled by seeing several on the daily walks with the dogs that have replaced our hunting trips.

Recently they have been quite scarce in the vicinity – possibly the result of the lepine equivalent of myxomatosis – but they are now recovering. But all this is, of course, just another daydream, frustration making it even more far-fetched than usual.

Hunting rabbits is more challenging, I'm sure. Can we catch them far enough away from their holes? Will the bird spot them? If he does, will he fly them? Is the rabbit going to jink at the last moment into that nettle patch? Where is the inevitable bolt hole hidden – the one which will thwart the bird at the last moment when success looks inevitable? I want the scales to be tilted, if at all, in the quarry's favour, not the bird's. It seems far more exciting.

In any event this is all academic. Rabbits are far easier to obtain permission to hunt than hares. As the traveller who sold me Bracken observed: 'I wish the dogs wouldn't bring back hares. I like eating them, but they're more trouble than they're worth. If your dogs catch rabbits farmers don't give a toss, but hares are game – people care about them.'

Thursday 6 May

IT SEEMS IRONIC that with the hawk grounded he is occupying increasing amounts of my time rather than less. Thinking and writing about him seems a natural therapy to cope with the frustration. Roll on the end of the moult!

In the interim, however, I content myself with watching the local kestrel, visiting falconry centres and pestering Jack. The frustration, however, has given me an idea about moulting Sioux free the next year. It springs from a description of a red tail that was set free every spring, content to hang around its keeper's farm, fed occasionally, but living mainly off the resident pigeons which it caught for itself. In theory this feat is completely beyond a buzzard, but apparently she would open her wings every time the doves tried to land on the farm roof. Off they would flutter to circle the buildings before repeating the attempt. Again the hawk would open its wings and off they'd go. By nightfall the poor pigeons would be exhausted and sufficiently inured to the apparently harmless hawk to lower their guard.

This has firmly planted the idea of a free moult in my mind. It was strengthened when I read that one of the red tail's 'faults' is to be very territorial. Once in adult plumage, it becomes not only very attached to its home base but also very possessive. To the American mind, this is a problem. Red tails are the commonest raptor there and used as the beginner's bird. Being so common and so mammal-oriented, they are not rated very highly and present a problem when it comes to moving to the next bird. If the red tail is given away to another falconer within a radius of a hundred miles or so they are liable to return and if, on arriving back 'home', it discovers another bird on the lawn it will attempt to kill it.

The territorial nature of the red tail is, of course, not a problem to my plan. On the contrary it is an added attraction. Unlikely to wander far, Sioux will be able to sit on top of the house, getting as much exercise as he wants – coincidentally saving me a fair amount of time cleaning out his pen – and giving me the pleasure of seeing him fly during the enforced pause in hunting him.

I am again drifting into ludicrous daydreams, but ignoring the practical problems my fantasy wanders on, pondering the theoretical difficulties. What, for example, if Sioux were to become a father?

Judging from the newsletter of the British Falconers'

Club, the question of hybrid birds is the biggest issue dividing serious falconers today. The various species of raptors are, comparatively speaking, very closely related. Not only can two completely different species produce viable offspring, but in some cases the progeny are fertile. The purists argue that there is a risk of producing the genetic equivalent of the mink and grey squirrel catastrophes.

Personally, I believe the argument to be ridiculous. Hybrids have never been recorded in the wild, in spite of the frequent overlap of species. Gyrs and peregrines occur in most of Canada, for example, while there are three buteos spread across Europe and ten in North America, to say nothing of subspecies (fourteen of the red tail alone).

Nevertheless, there is always the worry that were the moulting Sioux to meet wild native buzzards, he might pair up with a female. Theoretically he could produce offspring which would, in turn, breed with others, adding red tail genes to the make up of common buzzards. Quite rightly, this would be greeted as an environmental disaster. I reckon there's little danger of a pairing, however. For the next couple of years he will be sexually immature and thus I can keep an eye on his behaviour without any risk. Anyway, I won't turn him loose until late March or early April, long after any local birds have paired up, and if there were to be any sign of courtship displays I could easily take him back up.

It is, of course, a ludicrous scheme in every respect: another pipe-dream born out of my frustration as I took the dogs for a walk in the place of the hawk.

Saturday 8 May

IN THEORY I am supposed to be writing an article on waste management, but there seems little chance of any progress today, due to the wonderful sight behind the computer screen. A musket is on the fence post barely twenty yards away. He has just flashed down the hedge, rocketing along the side of the tangle of bramble and elder. In his foot is a tiny corpse – I think it's a blue tit – and he seems to be about to pluck it.

As he stands there, his tiny, orange-barred chest heaving rapidly with the exertion of explosive flight, I can barely breathe. Sparrowhawks may be comparatively common around here, but you still don't see them every day. He seems confident and his head dips towards the breast of the unfortunate tit. With deft flicks of his beak the yellow feathers begin to float down towards the grass below. My heart is pounding and throat tight. This is one of the most exciting moments of nature-watching I have ever had.

Yet, apart from the rarity of such a sight, why am I so thrilled? Field sportsmen all too often claim that hunting is an instinctive urge, an activity as old as humankind itself. Man (and here they usually mean the male) is a hunter who provides protein for the table by pursuing and killing quarry, returning to dump it triumphantly in front of the family group.

This is only partially true. Hunting, particularly when armed with the tools of the Stone Age, is time-consuming and usually inefficient. Man's urge to kill is instinctive, but weak. Much stronger is the urge to chase and be chased. This can be found in playgrounds around the world, regardless of industrialisation, diet or religion. Games based on the principle of pursuit – hunting as opposed to killing – are universal, be they 'tag' or 'hide-and-seek'. These are tamer, but recognisable versions of falconry, a sport which dates back to the earliest civilisations and certainly overlaps the arrival of Europe's first hunter gatherers by a millennia or two.

The tiny hunter has now almost finished his task of plucking the unfortunate tit and a dusting of fluff is still hanging in the air around the post, floating ever so slowly downwards in the warmth of the afternoon. Will he eat it here or has he a mate sitting on eggs nearby? I don't know which I'd prefer more . . . but as I try to weigh up the options he's gone, off as quickly as he arrived. Perhaps he saw me or heard the keys clicking away. In any event, there is now no more sign of him than the feathers drifting down, and even they have almost all gone. The whole incident took little more than a minute, but I can tell it has ruined any prospect of work for the rest of the day. How can I possibly analyse the latest techniques for the disposal of the detritus of modern life when I've just seen that? What importance can it possibly have? For the time being, the article seems totally trivial and banal.

Sunday 9 May

AFTER SEEING THE sparrowhawk my composure was so rattled that I gave up and turned the television on in an attempt to let the memory fade. The sound drifted out before the picture emerged and I caught the unmistakable terminology of the hunt.

'Oh, he's kicked his heels now,' came a voice.

'He's drawing away, the gap is growing,' it continued, its tone rising in excitement. It was an athletics race, a sport in which I have absolutely no interest, but for once I listened entranced.

As the runner neared the line I smiled as I recognised in his tone the baying of a dog in hot pursuit. 'He's clean away,' screamed the voice in an ecstasy of excitement. 'They'll never catch him now!!!'

Even at the best of times, athletics holds little fascination for me and after a few minutes I turned the thing off in disgust. My mind still filled with the hawk, I drove into the town to check up on the progress of the local gunsmith. He has been looking at my old air rifle with a view to replacing its ancient spring and adjusting the bent barrel. The news was bad. Wearily shaking his head, he told me it was past repair.

Instead he managed to sell me a secondhand gun. I bought it ostensibly to keep young visitors happy, but primarily for myself, hoping to enjoy 'plinking' at targets and tin cans in the garden. I also wanted something powerful enough to shoot the occasional crow or jackdaw (in the past I would have added rabbit and squirrel to the list, but this is now out of the question, being reserved entirely for the hawk). I thought that stalking the all-too-frequent magpies might sate my hunting spirit, reduce the pressure on the local songbird population and provide me with a pair of wings to make a lure for the falcon plan that I'm still toying with.

I was wrong. I have just discovered how much I have changed since, as a teenager, I crept along local hedgerows looking for sparrows and starlings to feed to the ferrets. Then, I used to dream of bagging a rabbit, the equivalent to my childhood imagination of a tiger to a Victorian big game-hunter. Things seem different now that I'm an adult. No doubt the local magpies need controlling: with almost no natural predators around here they have proliferated. 'One for sorrow, two for joy . . .' goes the nursery rhyme, but the numbers stop at ten, obviously composed at a time or place when there were fewer to be seen. Once last winter I caught sight of a flock more reminiscent of rooks than their smaller cousins. A cloud of them rose from a field as I drove home, flying alongside the car, wings flashing white, black and metallic blue. Too many to count for certain, there must have been at least twenty, far bigger than a family group.

Attractive, intelligent birds, magpies take a dreadful toll of eggs and nestlings. Indeed I can see this every time I sit at the computer. Fifty yards away from the window a pair of collared doves are nesting in a hawthorn thicket. They may be classified as a pest, but they are beautiful birds, a lovely shade of pinky-brown, a little slash of black across their necks. They are canny creatures too, rarely flying straight to their nest, but alighting in a nearby ash to check the coast is clear before flitting quickly into the bush.

Their caution is well-justified. There are several magpies around and they know there are pickings somewhere around the hawthorn. A couple of days ago one was mobbed around the ash by the dove which put on a ferocious display for such a tiny symbol of peace. Smaller and almost defenceless in comparison with the powerfully-beaked scavenger, the little bird nevertheless had the determination to drive it off, but in the long run it is clear that its pluck has only alerted the magpie. Ever since it keeps returning to the area, hopping around the bushes, peering upwards in search of the nest it knows must be there.

I decided to do something to help: I tossed this morning's bacon rind out on to the shed roof. Sure enough the magpies were soon eating it in the field in front of the window, well within range. One in particular kept returning and presented an easy target. But I did nothing – I couldn't bring myself to kill it. I might shoot rats without compunction, but somehow it seemed unfair to kill the bird as it ate – the more so because it was I who had fed it. Anyway, it too might have a nest somewhere and to save a dove squab so that a magpie chick starved seemed an unsatisfactory swap. My inability to shoot the magpie gives me a wholly irrational sense of impotence and guilt. At the same time it has filled me with an ironic fury at other field sports. Why should I feel guilt at not shooting a bird which, were Sioux capable of it, I would be only too delighted to see in his claws?

The failure also only serves to remind myself of why I am so obsessed. The pleasure of falconry is perhaps best conveyed in a minor classic, *Laggard*, written by one of the last of his breed, Ronald Stevens – a country squire who spent his summers and autumns on the moors, hunting grouse with peregrines with the aid of his falconer, a few selected friends and his dogs. He described the appeal as:

> The privilege of a spectator to one of Nature's performances that, for sheer drama, cannot be surpassed. My part of the show is over and done with before the falcon stoops, for it is in the hours of training her that I have really been after that grouse.
>
> Occasionally I see the wild peregrine execute her own brilliant stoop at the same quarry and that I find even more thrilling, if possible . . . Is it shameful to stand and admire the wonderful power in flight, the speed and the skill with which the falcon secures her legitimate prey? Hawking will always go on in the wild, no jealous person can stop that. Whether the hawk hunts for herself or for man she will always show sport in the highest sense of that inspiring word. No one but a complete Pharisee would deliberately lower his eyes to the ground when the peregrine falcon stoops.

The words are overblown, there is more than a hint of the self-righteous, but nevertheless he puts into words sentiments which sum up my total obsession. I fly Sioux solely for the pleasure of seeing the flight of the hunter. As Stevens points out, the real thing will always be better and, were Sioux to be free, hunting wild rather than living off the offal of urban egg-eaters, he would do exactly the same thing.

Once loose, he flies according to instinct alone. It is my privilege to be allowed to watch him try to outwit his quarry. If it escapes, good luck to it: tomorrow it will have to pit its wits against fox, stoat, badger and mink, to say nothing of the biggest threat of all – man.

It is chiefly because of the thought of seeing him fly that I have just put my Islington flat on the market. I am not sure what I shall do or where I shall go, but I am almost certain that I can't return to London. Maybe I can find something around here, possibly something to the west, I can't decide.

Monday 10 May

THE LITTLE OWL that nested in the ivy-covered stump at the end of the lane last year has returned. It is not the only owl in the area. I caught a glimpse of something brown on my way back from the pub – almost certainly a tawny owl – and, much more exciting, the night before last I saw the ghostly white form of a barn owl crossing the road above the cottage. It has been ten years since I last spotted one around here and it was wonderful to see its pale shape floating silently across the road.

Coincidentally, the sight of all these owls came just in time for one of the village children. This afternoon, when I let the dogs out to empty themselves, to my dismay the two older animals went haring around the house, barking wildly. I tore after them, cursing their noise and hoping that whoever it was on the other side would not be too frightened by the bared teeth and aggression.

There I found Caroline, the woman who months ago had been so disgusted by the hawk's diet of chicks. She and her daughter Sophie were cowering against Sioux's enclosure. We all started apologising profusely, Caroline about venturing into the garden without permission (she thought I was out) while I grovelled about the dogs, whose barks had reduced Sophie to tears.

With the apologies readily accepted on both sides, Caroline explained her daughter was doing a school project on owls and she had thought I might have one in addition to the hawk. They were looking for pellets and feathers to illustrate the ten-minute talk that the nine-year-old was to give to her class. I went into the pen to fetch a casting, but had to point out that it wouldn't be too interesting, being the remains of day-old chicks and little more than powdery yellow dust.

I suggested that they walk to the end of the lane to where I'd seen the little owl. Caroline looked blank, so I offered to show her the spot. I felt guilty about the snivels that were still shuddering through the child. As we walked I told them where the three local species are to be found – the little owl outside the cottage, the tawnies in the copse and the barn owl a couple of hundred yards in the opposite direction.

She asked whether the decline in the last was due to all the conversions of farm buildings around here. I told her, I hope truthfully, that modern agriculture was the main problem. After all, I pointed out, barn owls were not invented when man first built storehouses for his crops. To add to my conviction, the only roosting or nesting owls I have ever seen around here have been in hollow trees. There are plenty of these around and the owls have used them for generations as breeding-sites.

When we arrived at the tree, I knocked down the lacy heads of the cow parsley and nettles, dropping to my knees to search the ground. I had little hope of finding anything, but with so many nettles and both women bare-legged and not knowing what to look for, I felt I had to make the effort.

To my surprise I immediately found not one but four pellets. Each tiny bundle grey with mouse fur and flecked with the shiny black of beetle shells. Both size and contents indicated little owls.

Better still, on the return walk I found a feather in a second hollow tree. It was soft and silky, flecked brown, white and grey. In this case I was less certain, but given its location, felt reasonably sure that it was also an owl's. The two left very pleased with the success of their walk and I too felt satisfied with the act of a good Samaritan, to say nothing of looking extremely knowledgeable: a real countryman.

Wednesday 12 May

THE WEEK BEGAN in a devastating way for me. After a relaxing weekend and productive Monday, I got up yesterday and turned on the computer to warm up while getting dressed. As I pulled on my socks I heard the dreaded 'Peep!' from the machine that means all is not well. Repeated attempts merely produced the same result. The beast was insistent: 'Give me the date and time and insert a system disk.'

Like so many of my generation I am now dependent on the word processor. It is my friend and the tool of my trade. And if my dependence on the machine is typical, so is my inability to comprehend what makes it work. As a result, when it failed to obey my commands, a strange sense of irrational panic took over. The throat tightened, my stomach churned and I felt physically sick. Everything else became unimportant – even the hawk was temporarily forgotten – and my world centred, briefly, on the grey plastic box lurking on the table upstairs.

As I stared balefully at the blank screen, I knew I was helpless and panicked. It was made all the more disturbing by the knowledge that I had no copies of the last two weeks' work – twelve-thousand painstaking words – and not even a printed version.

Fortunately, however, I located someone in London who could fix the fault, although I had to spend all night – literally – driving to and from the capital. He was dubious about whether he could solve the problem, but discovered the fault within the first ten minutes. The next three hours were spent working on the machine, wiping parts of the hard disk and sorting out various glitches that he assured me were there, but of whose existence, until that point, I had been blissfully unaware. Although I had been happy with my machine's performance prior to the crash and he was charging me by the hour for his labour, I let him get on with it, grateful that the thing was working once more and that my file was safe. It wasn't until half-past four that I got to bed.

The whole incident reminds me of the central irony that has crept into my life. While totally dependent on the latest technology, I am practising one of the oldest sports known to man and considering a further retreat from the modern world: a flight to somewhere even more remote than here. I can see the headline of an article now: 'Falconry leads to telecommuting.'

By this morning I had recovered from the shock and was about to start work when the dogs went wild in the lane. A loud and unmistakable cry rang out, accompanied by the swish of wings. Two peacocks were being herded down the lane by Graham and his daughter and the commotion had scared them into flight. Sure enough there they were, a cock and a hen balanced precariously in the branches of the old apple trees in the orchard below the cottage. Surprisingly Graham was not bothered by the dogs, but resigned. He'd bought the birds two days ago and ever since had been chasing them around the countryside. He complained in his falsetto voice that until they disappeared, he'd no idea they were able to fly.

It was an amusing way to start a day which turned out to be unproductive in most respects. I got little writing done and failed to finish a review before I set off for Oxford to do my weekly washing. If I was feeling depressed about the writing block, however, the mood disappeared rapidly during the drive. Turning on to the main road above the village, I caught a glimpse of a slate grey bird powering across the main road. Although I have never seen one before, I was in no doubt about its identity. With its coloration, style of flight

179

and unmistakable raptor's sense of purpose it had to be a hobby.

These are summer migrants to Britain, miniature peregrines which hunt insects and small birds up to the size of, and including, swifts. The books say they are rare, with only a hundred pairs or so nesting here every year, but this seems unlikely. Bill, the old naturalist who lives in the town, says they are relatively common locally – at least during the summer. But like many raptors, they are very difficult to spot unless you know what to look for. He cites the case of an experienced bird-watching friend of his who had a nest within a couple of hundred yards of his house. He was completely oblivious to its existence until another birder spotted it – and by this stage the eyasses were 'branchers', almost fully-feathered and venturing out along the tree's limbs.

He has only one acquaintance who is good at spotting these scimitar-winged hunters: and he only manages this with lengthy winter research. Apparently they invariably rear their young in an old crow's nest and Bill's friend carefully notes the presence of every possible local site when they are easy to spot amid the bare branches. He returns the next summer, waiting for long hours near each site, hoping to see a parent returning with food, either for its mate or growing youngsters.

The sighting reminded me of *The Goshawk*. Set during the summer of 1937, the book didn't appear until 1951. The reason for this, according to White, was his discovery of a hobbies' nest. He was unwilling to cut the discovery out of his text, but was worried that if he published, unscrupulous men might disturb the birds. A training camp during the war caused the birds to quit, however, and thus he felt able to go to press, fourteen years after he had sat there quietly, 'waking' gos, scribbling in pencil through the long night hours, bird perched on his left fist.

The disturbance he feared most was from egg collectors who were then still common. Fortunately today there are few practitioners of this nineteenth-century mania, but reading the press you might think that they had been replaced by falconers as the bogey men of the conservation world.

Anyone who understands the sport today could tell them this is rubbish – but still the stories circulate of peregrines being worth thousands of pounds in the Gulf and of their nests being under constant risk of plunder by unscrupulous falconers. Such allegations simply don't bear examination. To begin with, the Arabs – some of the world's most dedicated falconry practitioners – don't rate the peregrine. For them, sakers and gyrs are the pinnacle of their art. More importantly, however, a captive-bred peregrine tiercel is worth about £300 today and a falcon £500. Fairly pricey granted, but acquiring one doesn't involve dangling over a cliff on a thin piece of rope, risking detection by anyone within sight of the nest (and these are usually visible over a very large area). Even supposing the raider were to manage to grasp an eyass without frightening it into its first uncertain flight, without a Department of the Environment ring the bird is, if not worthless, almost impossible to sell.

This is a 'close ring' – a seamless band of metal etched with an official number, into which the bird's foot grows. Once on, the hawk wears it for life. The ring can only be fitted when the eyass is about ten days old – before that it will fall off and a couple of days later the foot is too big to allow it to slide on. Ownership of an unringed bird, let alone its sale, is illegal except in exceptional cases.

The suggestion that Britain's raptors are under threat from falconers becomes even more implausible when one considers that only three of Britain's twenty or so species of raptors have any significant monetary value – at least to falconers. Priciest is the goshawk, incidentally, a bird which was re-established in Britain by falconers, after an absence of a century, at about a thousand pounds each. Peregrines are worth at most half that, while the tiny merlin is the third, worth roughly the same as a peregrine tiercel. Sparrowhawks and buzzards are of limited use: and anyway, are so common and easy to breed in captivity that they are frequently literally given away. Of the three valuable species, probably only the gos would be worth the hassle of theft from the wild.

All right, say the critics, but some people are still unwilling to pay the price and will take what they won't pay for. They are right, but in such cases it makes far more sense to raid a breeder than risk one's life for at best two or three unrung wild chicks. One night's work could net a thief dozens of close-rung eyasses – and their parents too. When one considers that a relatively small-scale local breeder I know has, in his words: 'thirty or forty birds, I'm not quite sure, to tell you the truth', one can see that depleting wild stocks is of little appeal to someone after a quick buck.

The most serious falconry threat to wild birds comes in the form of the enthusiastic amateur – usually a teenager like Billy in Barry Hines's *Kes* – who spots a nest and, on impulse, raids it to try his hand at the sport. Such opportunism is to be decried (the more so because it almost invariably involves one of the smallest – and thus most unsuitable – birds for the beginner), but its impact is limited to an individual bird, not the species concerned. In general the sport can hardly be considered a threat to wild birds – after all the sight of someone flying any hawk, let alone an illegal one, is not exactly an everyday event.

Falconry has existed for thousands of years. Throughout that time birds have been taken from the wild – indeed until a generation ago no one even bothered to breed them in captivity – yet wild populations stayed constant. Even today hundreds of raptors change hands in the Lahore bird markets every year, and the commonly-traded sakers and goshawks are still two of the most widely distributed raptors.

The threats to the world's raptors comes from other directions, by far the most important being habitat destruction and persistent pesticides. In this country, however, the dangers are of a different nature. Poisoning and shooting, whether accidental or deliberate, are the biggest direct check on numbers. Mind you, things have improved since the last century when anything with a hooked beak was destroyed on sight. Today only a handful of people resent the presence of raptors – the most dangerous being a few Neanderthal gamekeepers and farmers – and as a result it is reckoned that there are now more raptors in Britain than at any point this century. Kestrels have never been so common – and if the population growth of peregrines after the DDT tragedy of the Fifties and Sixties has now stopped, it is limited only by numbers saturating every suitable site.

It is thus doubly ironic that today one of the most vociferous groups calling for raptor control are British bird enthusiasts. Pigeon fanciers, particularly around the Severn estuary and South Wales, have been lobbying for local peregrines to be controlled, either by shooting or trapping for release elsewhere. Some have even gone to the ludicrous extreme of proposing to rig explosive charges to their birds in the hope that they take their killer with them.

The problem is that peregrines are killing and eating their prize racing-birds, choosing by preference domestic pigeons over their cousins, because homers fly higher and with less deviation than wild or feral birds. As a result, a falcon has merely to reach its pitch high above one of the former mining valleys, waiting for birds to return to their lofts. Under attack the domestic bird has none of the native wit of the wood-pigeon or stock dove. Instead it merely flies home faster, allowing the falcon to put in two or even three stoops. If some long-buried instinct comes to the surface and the bird dives for cover, its altitude puts it at a disadvantage, giving the hunter a greater opportunity to make a successful strike.

The predation is exacerbated by 'wedding'. In the wild falcons tend to specialise in one species over all others. Peregrines are particularly prone to this, in Britain normally choosing grouse, seabirds or pigeons. The last is one of the most challenging quarries a falcon could pick: fast, manoeuvrable and canny birds, rarely far from cover and safety. (Indeed the difficulty of the hunt is sufficient to make all but the most foolhardy of falconers go to great lengths to discourage their birds from chasing them: it leads to a trial of stamina, covers many miles and, sooner or later, results in a lost bird.)

Domestic pigeons are different, however. Their height and unswerving flight allows the falcons to hunt more enclosed land than would otherwise be the case. With the wild peregrine population at saturation point, it is not surprising that several pairs have taken to preying exclusively on homing birds.

Top racing pigeons can be worth thousands of pounds and owners complain bitterly, particularly when many of them do it full-time. They live in areas where the last of the jobs have long since gone and former miners and steel workers are faced with a lifetime on the dole. I sympathise with their love of animals and the hopelessness of their plight when faced with a society which no longer cares, but this is one fight with authority where I am on the other side.

Pigeons are such unappealing birds. Made to run away, to live in perpetual fear of the predator, gregarious creatures that flock together to minimise the risks of being picked out by the hunter. How can anyone compare a pigeon with a falcon? It's like asking someone – which is more impressive, a Reliant Robin or a Ferrari? Were I a pigeon fancier, I would happily accept the losses merely for the honour of sharing a neighbourhood with these kings of the sky. No, I'd go further and wait at the head of the valley when the birds were due to return, hoping to see the falcon's strike – the higher, the steeper, the more powerful the better. To catch a glimpse of a wild peregrine making a kill would be priceless.

And on a more prosaic note, the idea of selectively culling peregrines or shipping them out of the area just wouldn't work. The population of wild peregrines is at saturation point. Shoot one and another would take its place. Shoot that and the same thing would happen again. It would be the same rut that almost led to the extermination of most of our medium-sized predators last century. Heavily-preserved estates would kill everything that threatened the pheasants or partridges. As the numbers of hunters dropped, game would increase temporarily, only to act as a magnet to predators on neighbouring land. These would be shot in turn – and so on.

The other suggestion – of shipping trapped peregrines to release points far away – is, if anything, more ridiculous. The falcon may not be capable of the same feats of homing as a pigeon, but as its name denotes, it is a wanderer, covering hundreds or even thousands of square miles in the course of a year. There is every chance that a released peregrine would return – particularly if it had bred successfully in the locality.

The fanciers ignore the fact that the underlying problem lies with their birds. These are the interlopers. It is they who have been bred to behave artificially and it is this which makes them easy meat for falcons. As long as peregrines overlap with pigeons, they will prey on them. Given that some races cover hundreds of miles, if you were to eliminate any falcon that might present a threat, you would have to exterminate every British peregrine. With them would go two-thirds of Europe's population of the species.

The fanciers should cut their losses and revel in what must be one of nature's greatest flying displays. Better still, provided the victim is not one of their prize birds, the whole thing is free too!

I pondered all this as I sped along, but then had more fuel for thought as I caught sight of the brown flecked underside of a bird flying across the road ten miles further on. Again it was unmistakably a hawk, but appeared too large to be a female sparrowhawk, to say nothing of the colouring being wrong. I thought, but couldn't be certain, that it was a tiercel goshawk. But by the time I reached Oxford only ten minutes later, I had convinced myself that it was. The very thought made me weak with excitement. Much as I love watching Sioux hunt, I would give my eye teeth to see a wild goshawk kill. It is not for nothing that it is rated as the pinnacle of hawking. No, as White was all too well aware, a goshawk has everything an austringer could require. It is superbly efficient, with a phenomenal turn of speed and, to add to its appeal, is beautiful. Even the uninitiated can see that it is every inch a killer, its eyes yellow in youth, orange and then red in old age, seem permanently flared. It looks almost indignant at the affrontery of a human daring to feast his eyes on it. In adult plumage its blue-grey feathers, pale stomach barred with black and long, elegant legs with their large, powerful feet, have a grace and beauty that catch the attention of any observer.

I told Jack about it when I phoned to arrange a visit to see his eyasses. He was pleased, but not surprised. He said he'd deliberately released a lot around Oxfordshire.

'Of course the RSPB will get all the credit, but it's us falconers that are responsible,' he said in his gap-toothed, slurring way. 'That lot are useless, they do bugger all for raptors!'

Unfortunately two of his three peregrine chicks have failed to survive. One merely pipped the shell before dying while the other one managed to struggle free of its egg, only to perish the next day. I was sympathetic. Suddenly a note of suspicion crept into his voice.

'You're not hooked are you?' he said. I laughed, but he seemed serious. 'Watch out, it's highly addictive and very easy to waste a great deal of time. I'm almost sixty and have been flying hawks for thirty-five years. Sometimes I look back and wonder what happened to my life.' He was only partially joking, with a genuine note of sorrow in his voice.

As normally happens in conversations with Jack, the talk began to ramble and I returned to the subject of a second bird. The frustration of the moult has become totally unbearable and I'd decided to go ahead with the purchase of a falcon: a 'bird of the lure' rather than the fist, like Sioux. But this still left me with the problem of which bird to pick, a peregrine or a saker?

He thought that a tiercel would be the best bet. These are easy to train and, more importantly, enter. In contrast sakers can be very awkward and are inclined to migrate around October. This, he pointed out, can lead to one looking pretty foolish. The advantage of the tiercel over the falcon is that it is more manoeuvrable and even quicker to hunt than its sister.

Although I still cherish the vague hope that he will give me one of his birds, I could hardly ask him for a gift. So, by way of a slight hint, I explained that for complicated reasons a Suffolk breeder owed me money which we had agreed would count as the first hundred pounds towards a bird. The mention of money brought a reprimand from him.

'Never, never mix money and birds,' he said. 'I've told you that before – and you just don't listen, do you? You may have to pay for a bird – God knows you have to pay for everything nowadays – but it isn't an investment. It's a beautiful creature – it isn't worth anything!'

I agreed with him. I couldn't do anything else. At first when I flew Sioux I too had thought of him as an investment worth £425, flapping away from me, potentially lost every time he flew. But gradually, as the season progressed, the sheer joy of watching him fly took over. To watch him hurtle across a valley after a rabbit, to see him flap up laboriously, into the uppermost branches of a tree, or to hurtle, wings closed, on to my fist – these are all-important. This is why I dream of seeing him riding a thermal or moulting free. I no longer care if he is mine to possess and control: now the only importance of his return is so that I can repeat the experience tomorrow.

As we talked Jack was clearly becoming enthused by my interest: 'Look,' he said, 'My saker had two clutches of four eggs each. I've given three of the first to a friend who's a sort of partner, but the peregrines are fostering the remaining one in the hope it will encourage them next year. I had to give their chick to a friend who wants to imprint it for breeding purposes.' The news that he had no peregrines to give away was a blow to my hopes that he might give me a bird, but these were given a lift by the slight hesitation in his voice which followed, as if something had occurred to him. 'Look, why don't you come over and see the eyass?'

Naturally I jumped at the opportunity, perhaps he was thinking of giving me a saker instead? The thought has now produced its own problem. The visit wasn't for another five days and I find myself counting away the hours with a growing sense of impatience. If he doesn't believe in selling birds, but he knows I am desperate to have one, could he be going to give me one? Again my imagination is running riot. I mean, how many people can there be in Britain who would want a saker? Rationally I know he must have a huge range of falconry friends, but who knows, perhaps . . .

Thursday 13 May

THE FRUSTRATION has been broken in part by the sight of Sioux's first tail feathers coming through. This means that the moult is progressing well, although Jack has warned me I would be very lucky to have him hunting before the beginning of August. I am less convinced. I've never seen a moult before, but he seems to be shedding his feathers very rapidly. It is still clear, however, that it will be at least another six weeks before I can possibly fly him again.

But the sight of his new feathers has another fascination for me. Red tails are so named for fairly obvious reasons. In their first year, like many raptors, they are so-called 'brown hawks': a uniform drab muddy colour. Once in adult plumage, however, the reason for the name becomes apparent as the new tail emerges. Ever since his arrival I have been curious to see quite what this is going to look like – with fourteen subspecies of the bird, there is a huge variation in tail colours and I was fervently hoping that it was not the same traffic-cone orange of that on display in my hawk video.

Fortunately, however, from the tiny shoot emerging from beneath his folded wings, it looks as if it is going to be a rusty cinnamon shade. Obviously this has absolutely no effect on his hunting ability, but the beauty of the birds has always been no small part of the joy of falconry. After all, the pure white gyr falcons of the high Arctic have always commanded fantastic prices, with medieval kings of England spending thousands of pounds (millions in modern values) on equipping expeditions to capture just one good cast of the creatures.

When I went to see Jack he was his normal affable, but slightly absent-minded self. The major subject of our conversation was, predictably, the falcon. Jack was now earnestly advising getting a saker, contradicting his earlier advice. The reason was that as we talked through possible quarry species it became obvious that crows and rooks were the only realistic possibility. Although a peregrine can cope with a rook, the tiercels find it a tough fight and crows are a struggle even for a big falcon. As a result he thought I should go for a saker – 'Might as well hit 'em with a cannon if you're going to go for them at all,' he said with one of his toothless grins.

In addition, unlike the peregrine, in the wild sakers hunt a fair amount of ground game, and in consequence are more useful in a tussle with a crow.

'They're bolshie bastards – like me, that's probably why I like them so much,' he laughed. 'The falcon equivalent of a goshawk, one moment they're fine with you and half a dozen spectators, the next day, for no apparent reason, they hate your guts and won't do anything.'

The saker has another drawback, however: a disconcerting habit of migrating in the autumn. 'I should know about that, I've lost half-a-dozen of the bastards – probably because I fly them so high,' said Jack ruefully, but then he perked up. 'And good luck to 'em.' He cackled.

In some ways the advice is a pity. Peregrines are such beautiful creatures and I was already more than a little hooked on the idea of owning one of these noble falcons. Grouse hawking with them is, after all, the pinnacle of European falconry, but like almost all falconers, I have to recognise that it is beyond my resources. To do it properly you need to spend a minimum of two months a year flying the birds solidly at grouse. To find these, I would need access to a well-stocked moor – way, way, beyond my pocket – and a trained dog, preferably a pointer, to find and mark the coveys. Even the lesser alternative of partridges is beyond my resources – with neither suitable land, nor the money to hunt them around here.

I should be realistic, Jack advised me, and go for a saker. My heart jumped as I thought he was about to offer me the bundle of fluff that was sitting with its peregrine foster parents. For a glorious moment I imagined that his change of advice was solely to justify giving me the eyass. My pulse raced, my eyes lit up and then, as quickly as my hopes had risen, they were dashed by his next comment: 'Better still, get

189

a saker/peregrine hybrid,' he said. 'They combine the virtues of the peregrine's instinctive hunting and the saker's power and pugnaciousness. I've got a friend who'll sell you one.'

With the realisation that he wasn't going to give me the bird, it became clear that it had been a fantasy from the first. He might not believe in selling birds, he might even like me, but he wasn't just going to hand over one of the five precious eyasses he'd bred this year. There may be no price tag attached to his birds, but this doesn't mean they are worthless. Instead, they are all the more valuable. He cares nothing for money and therefore can be even more discerning about where they end up, rather than less.

You might think that I was disappointed by this realisation, but in fact I found myself anything but. Conversations with another enthusiast are so rare and Jack is so nice that it would have been difficult to feel let down. In addition, his respect for the hybrids and his certainty that one of these would be so suited to my purposes impressed me enough that, by the end of the chat, had he offered me his eyass, I would have turned him down.

My enthusiasm was further fuelled by the realisation that it was one of these birds that I had seen flying at Newent. Not only was it beautiful, but it put on a spectacular display, disappearing from view in both height and distance from the crowd before returning at a phenomenal pace, stooping vertically from a couple of hundred feet at the lure being swung for it. Hurtling downwards, it appeared to be facing certain death, but just six feet above the ground, it pulled out of the dive, without checking its speed, judging it so finely that its trailing jesses brushed through the grass, flicking the heads of the daisies. The thought of owning one of these magnificent creatures was enough to send my pulse racing.

Unfortunately, however, when I rang up the breeder, he didn't have one. He told me, however, that a saker was definitely what I wanted. Not only was it bigger and tougher than a peregrine, but, oddly, was slightly more manoeuvrable and suited to Oxfordshire.

Disappointed, I phoned up my Suffolk breeder. He has

both sakers and peregrines available. At four and six hundred pounds for males and females respectively, they are over-priced, but at least I know he is reputable. He promised to reserve me one if I sent him a deposit. In passing I mentioned the £100 of mine that he'd said last year he'd offset against this year's bird.

'Remind me about it,' he said. I explained and he hummed a bit. 'It was a very long time ago,' he said reluctantly. 'Why don't we split the difference and call it £50?'

Surprised, I agreed, but now my blood is rising as I contemplate the proposed deal. While I don't mind paying for a bird, this is a falcon he is talking about, not a piece of machinery. I can't stop thinking of Jack's 'flying cheques' and am really irritated. There is something profoundly distasteful about his attitude, a mercenary edge that clashes with the nobility of a saker. I have now worked myself into quite a lather about the whole thing and have decided to buy else-where.

Tuesday 18 May

SIOUX'S RELUCTANCE TO have a bath has long been a source of worry. Most hawks are supposed to want to bathe daily, wading into the water with enthusiasm and positively looking forward to their morning tub. Ever since his arrival, however, he has shown a total lack of interest in washing himself, staring resentfully at the large earthenware cooking dish which acts as his bathtub. Every day I have religiously put the bowl out, filled with a tempting four inches of fresh, clean, water and every day he has studiously ignored its temptations.

This ought to be completely immaterial, of course. Whether or not he bathes has no impact on how he flies – in fact, if anything, it could be considered to be the reverse. Some hawks are so keen on bathing that they can be a pain, for it is impossible to fly them before they have had a dip: otherwise they will fly off on their own to find a suitable puddle for their routine ablutions.

Sioux's distaste for water should have been of no import, but in fact it has been an irritation. With only his beak to keep him clean and tidy, he has grown tatty, many feathers lacking their tips, tail feathers chalky with mutes. The problems are only exacerbated by his apparent preference for perching on the ground, his deck spread out on the grass behind him, its ends bent back against the grass.

So it was with some surprise that I found him wet last week, his legs and belly feathers bunched into dripping dark spikes. I suspected that he might have had a bath, but as a light drizzle had fallen all night, I thought it possible that this was just the product of one of the many leaks in the corrugated plastic roof.

My doubts were dispelled when I went out to check on him four days ago, to find him standing in the bowl, the water lapping against his vent feathers. He stared balefully at me, almost daring me to laugh at the undignified spectacle.

Instead I stood there breathlessly, watching as he slowly lowered first one shoulder and then the other into the cold water, rolling it in little rivulets across his back. Tatty or not, he is still incredibly beautiful, the glossy chocolate brown feathers on his back overlapping in a series of triangles, each feather edged in a lighter shade of brown – delicately etching out a chain mail in gold. As he dipped and rolled in the water, the droplets running along his backbone and disappearing into his tail, I felt like Solomon watching Bathsheba, revelling in the moment, but feeling furtive, almost guilty. I was a peeping Tom.

Having finished his dip, he flew up to the highest perch in the mews and sat there, still glowering. He was shivering slightly, in spite of the warmth of the room, bathed in the soft sunshine of a May morning.

Since then he seems to be taking regular dips – or at least he has deigned to bathe twice on particularly fine mornings. I am doubly glad about this because, according to Jack, during the moult bathing encourages the bird to preen itself, massaging the blood through the roots of the feathers and easing the new webbing out of its sheath.

'If he doesn't bathe himself you should spray him with a hose instead,' he said. 'But if he's doing it for himself once or twice a week that should do.'

If his ablutions are welcome, his dislike of the lawnmower is more of a problem. Having become distinctly wilder with his gain in weight, he is nevertheless still relatively tame when I enter his pen. The mower is another matter, however, and he bated incessantly whenever I mowed the grass outside his enclosure. Normally this would be all right – I could either move him on to his bow perch or ignore the tantrums inside the mews – but it is tricky during the moult. The new feathers are delicate and easily damaged if knocked and this could lead to problems the next hunting season.

Tuesday 1 June

THE HOLIDAY WEEKEND was a heavy one. My brother and his girlfriend came out to celebrate his birthday and the last of her qualifications as a solicitor. They had invited dozens of friends, many of whom stayed the night and it was a crowded two-day party. It was with mixed feelings that I opened up with hospitality what is now definitely 'home' to so many people. On the one hand it was nice to see many of them for the first time in ages, but on the other there was the disruption of my well-established routines. Worst of all, I think, was the noise of twenty people having fun, frolicking in the lengthening grass of the field next to the cottage, playing baseball while suffering from what one of them, a doctor, calls 'alcohol-induced deafness'.

But if this was a pain, it was sheer joy to be able to show the hawk to them. By cornering them one by one, I managed to talk about falconry almost non-stop for the whole weekend, swapping listeners every hour or so. Similarly I took parties out to see him, groups of respectful worshippers to my very own, private, God. And the effect was similar to the hushed silence that falls on an atheist walking into a cathedral. As they caught sight of him, voices would drop as their eyes drank in his every detail. With poor Bel having long since reached the point of hawk fatigue and now bordering on the brink of an exhausted collapse, it was bliss to be able to let loose on such an abundant audience.

The weekend also provided a useful insight into my own behaviour. For the past few months I had been living a cloistered existence, wrapped in the blanket of the Oxfordshire countryside, with hawk, dogs and ferret as my main company. Although of course I haven't been entirely deprived of human company – Bel, my parents and a handful of pub regulars all being important sources of social intercourse: they are used to my lifestyle and take it for granted.

I now realise quite how odd some of this must seem to outsiders. I was in the kitchen, chatting to Mike, a doctor, while attempting to cook nettle soup – my latest culinary discovery – and although he was not helping, at least I was grateful for the company. For once I was giving my voice a rest and allowing someone else to do the talking. He was holding forth on the importance of hygiene, looking suspiciously at the handfuls of unwashed nettles being crammed into the pressure cooker. In particular he said he hoped I had two sets of knives and chopping boards, one reserved for meat, the other for vegetables: cleanliness was so important. I said nothing, but couldn't help smiling as he picked at a piece of cake resting on a plate that, to my certain knowledge, had last been used to feed the ferret.

But the atmosphere changed abruptly when, absent-mindedly looking for a cold beer, he opened the freezer door. The cardboard box holding the hawk's food was half-open and there, sticking out like a railway signal, was a rat's tail.

His second glance took in the quail next to it and the chicks curled foetally around them. Now of course I am well aware that most people don't have rats, quails and dead chicks next to their frozen food, but then not everyone has a hawk. His reaction did seem a bit extreme however and it was doubly unfortunate that he should decide to rush next door to tell everyone. He should have anticipated the inevitable reaction of a load of drunks, particularly when there were two vegetarians in the room. Half the hawk's food supply for the next two months disappeared to be waved around the company, greeted by shrieks and roars of laughter.

It was all rather silly really. It is perfectly healthy: the chicks were too young to have picked anything up before being gassed and blast-frozen; quails are nice clean creatures and the rats were hygienically bred for the lab (even I would draw the line at putting farm or sewer rats next to my own food). Nevertheless it was a surprise to find how funny everyone found something that not only I, but even Bel and my parents, take for granted.

In general, however, I have tried to be quite careful about what I do. If I know visitors are coming who want to see Sioux I make sure there are no distressing cadavers on display. I buy in a bit of beef shin from the butcher's to demonstrate him on the fist. Nothing is achieved by pointlessly distressing people.

Wednesday 2 June

ALTHOUGH BY NOW the last of Sioux's first-year, brown tail feathers have gone, half the replacements have yet to grow. My frustration has reached such a pitch that there is nothing for it. I have just written the cheque for a saker. It is now three weeks old and will be ready in about a month's time. By then Sioux will almost be flying – but not quite. Thus, with a new bird I can squeeze in an extra three weeks falconry this year.

Best of all, I not only managed to locate a better bird than that of the Suffolk breeder, but it was also local – in fact one of Jack's, owned by his partner – and 'huge' by saker standards. It is more expensive than the other would have been, but money isn't the prime consideration. After my conversation with the breeder I had made up my mind to take the loss and find another bird.

It is difficult to overemphasise what this means. Most importantly I will now be able to fly a bird every day of the year. I can stagger their moults so Sioux begins in January or February and concentrate with the saker on crows until April or May. By then Sioux will be near enough ready to hunt again. The prospect is exhilarating.

It is also symbolic, the final nail in the coffin of any prospect that I might return to London. My flat might be on the market already, but until now it has been a move which is easily undone. When, last summer, I got Sioux, it was a careful choice, a hedging of bets. He might be a powerful bird, but as a buzzard he could be kept happily tethered in an Islington back garden during the week and flown at weekends. Given the uncertainties of my life at the time, it seemed safest to get a bird which could live and fly reasonably under peripatetic conditions.

But a falcon needs to work for its food. While a buzzard naturally 'stillhunts', a saker flies rapidly with fast wing beats, always on the qui vive. As a result it needs constant exercise to reach its peak. To keep a falcon in an Islington back garden would be an abomination.

And a saker would need space – lots of it. Even Oxford-shire – let alone London – is really too confined. By buying the falcon I am now totally committed not merely to a rural existence, but to a move to really wild country. Basically this means windswept moorland if I am to fly her properly. She means Wales or nothing.

There is no contest.

Bibliography

Beebe, F. L. and Webster, H. M.; *North American Falconry and Hunting Hawks* (World Press, Colorado, 1964): The best manual for US species (eg red tails), simply because American falconers have more experience of working with these raptors and are less encumbered with traditional methods devised for temperamental shortwings like goshawks.

Beebe, F. L.; *The Compleat Falconer* (Hancock House, 1992): A condensed update of *North American Falconry*.

Bodio, Stephen; *A Rage for Falcons* (Pruett, Boulder, 1992): Highly readable account by an American journalist/falconer of experiences ranging from capturing wild eyasses to imprinting and hunting.

Bert, Edmund; *An Approved Treatise of Hawkes and Hawking*, (1619): One of those classic texts that everyone cites and few read.

Ford, E.; *Falconry, Art and Practice* (Batsford, 1982): For all apart from Jack, this and Glasier are the two modern British texts.

Glasier, Phillip; *Falconry and Hawking* (Batsford, 1978): Although generally more thorough than Ford, this is less good on buzzards. It is still one of the two modern British canons.

Harting, J. E.; *Hints on the Management of Hawks and Practical Falconry* (1898): Descriptions of hawking from around the world at the turn of the century, including hunting wolves with golden eagles.

Longrigg, Roger; *The English Squire and His Sport* (Michael Joseph, 1977): A record of the changing pastimes of the aristocracy, with falconry taking a leading role until the reign of Charles I.

Marchington, John; *Pugs and Drummers* (Faber & Faber, 1978): Nothing to do with falconry, but it has a wonderful chapter on the history of the rabbit in the British Isles.

Mavrogodato, Jack; *A Hawk for the Bush* (H. F. & G. Witherby, 1960): The only austringer's manual in Jack's eyes.

Mitchell, E. B.; *The Art and Practice of Hawking* (Holland Press, 1987): According to Jack this is the only longwing book worth looking at, although it is rather old-fashioned.

Parry-Jones, Jemima; *Falcony, Care, Captive Breeding and Conservation* (David & Charles, 1988): An introduction to modern breeding techniques; it is fun to read and informative.

Stevens, Ronald; *Laggard* (Faber & Faber, 1953): A well-written account of falconry and its appeal by one of the last people in Britain to employ a professional falconer.

Stevens, Ronald; *Observations on Modern Falconry* (privately printed, 1957): A rather quirky manual on flying peregrines, with one of the best descriptions of the difficult art of hooding.

Upton, Roger; *Falconry, Principles and Practice* (A & C Black, 1991): Deals almost exclusively with peregrines, sakers and gyrs.

White, T. H.; *The Goshawk* (Cape, 1951): A literary masterpiece, despite White's antiquated techniques and frequent errors.

Woodford, M. H.; *A Manual of Falconry* (A & C Black, 1960): For a generation this was a standard training manual. Still worth looking at, if only to chart the changes in the sport over the last generation.

Most of these books are either difficult to get hold of or out of print, but many are available from:

Martin Jones
Falconry Furniture
The Parsonage
Llanrathal
Nr Monmouth
Monmouthshire NP5 3QJ

or

A bookshop which specialises in secondhand falconry works:

Nicholson's Prints and Books
6935 Shorecrest Drive
Anaheim, CA 92807 USA

The National Birds of Prey Centre near Newent in Gloucestershire (0531 820286) is probably the best of the many 'falconry centres' scattered around the countryside.

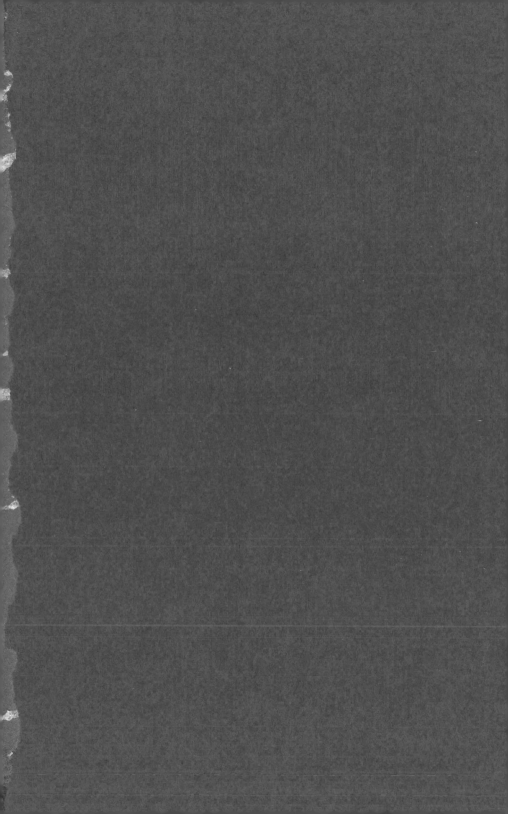